BLUEPRINTS

Religious Education
Key Stage 2
Copymasters

Ruth Parmiter

Monica Price

Stanley Thornes (Publishers) Ltd

Do you receive BLUEPRINTS NEWS?

Blueprints is an expanding series of practical teacher's ideas books and photocopiable resources for use in primary schools. Books are available for separate infant and junior age ranges for every core and foundation subject, as well as for an ever widening range of other primary teaching needs. These include **Blueprints Primary English** books and **Blueprints Resource Banks**. **Blueprints** are carefully structured around the demands of the National Curriculum in England and Wales, but are used successfully by schools and teachers in Scotland, Northern Ireland and elsewhere.

Blueprints provide:
- *Total curriculum coverage*
- *Hundreds of practical ideas*
- *Books specifically for the age range you teach*
- *Flexible resources for the whole school or for individual teachers*
- *Excellent photocopiable sheets – ideal for assessment and children's work profiles*
- *Supreme value.*

Books may be bought by credit card over the telephone and information obtained on **(01242) 577944**. Alternatively, photocopy and return this **FREEPOST** form to receive **Blueprints News**, our regular update on all new and existing titles. You may also like to add the name of a friend who would be interested in being on the mailing list.

Please add my name to the **BLUEPRINTS NEWS** mailing list.

Mr/Mrs/Miss/Ms _____

Home address _____

_____ Postcode _____

School address _____

_____ Postcode _____

Please also send **BLUEPRINTS NEWS** to:

Mr/Mrs/Miss/Ms _____

Address _____

_____ Postcode _____

To: Marketing Services Dept., Stanley Thornes Ltd, FREEPOST (GR 782), Cheltenham, GL50 1BR

Text © Ruth Parmiter and Monica Price 1994

Original line illustrations by Debbie Clark © ST(P) Ltd 1994

First published in 1994 by:
Stanley Thornes (Publishers) Ltd
Ellenborough House
Wellington Street
CHELTENHAM GL50 1YW

96 97 98 99 00 / 10 9 8 7 6 5 4 3

A catalogue record for this book is available from the British Library

0–7487–1645–9

Typeset by Tech-Set, Gateshead, Tyne & Wear
Printed and bound in Great Britain at The Bath Press, Avon

CONTENTS

INTRODUCTION

This book contains 90 photocopiable sheets that support many of the activities in the Teacher's Resource Book as well as the music and words for the nine songs. Where the copymasters are referred to in the text of the Teacher's Resource Book there are instructions on how to use them. They are referred to by number in the Teacher's Resource Book by this symbol:

.

The copymasters reinforce and extend activities in the Teacher's Resource Book in a wide range of cross-curricular ways. They develop skills to do with English, Science, Maths, Art and Geography (particularly mapping) but these skills are always used to develop clear RE objectives. Many of the copymasters help to introduce children to the major religions of the world.

Some of the sheets have particular scope for assessment and self-assessment of RE learning. You will find these sheets identified both in the Teacher's Resource Book and at the foot of the page by this logo:

.

These sheets will be particularly useful for building up a record of children's experiences in RE.

At the front of the book you will find the music and words for each of the nine songs that introduce the nine topics in **Blueprints** *Religious Education Key Stage 2*.

COPYMASTERS
i–ix
TOPIC SONGS

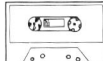

MY MIND

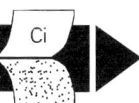

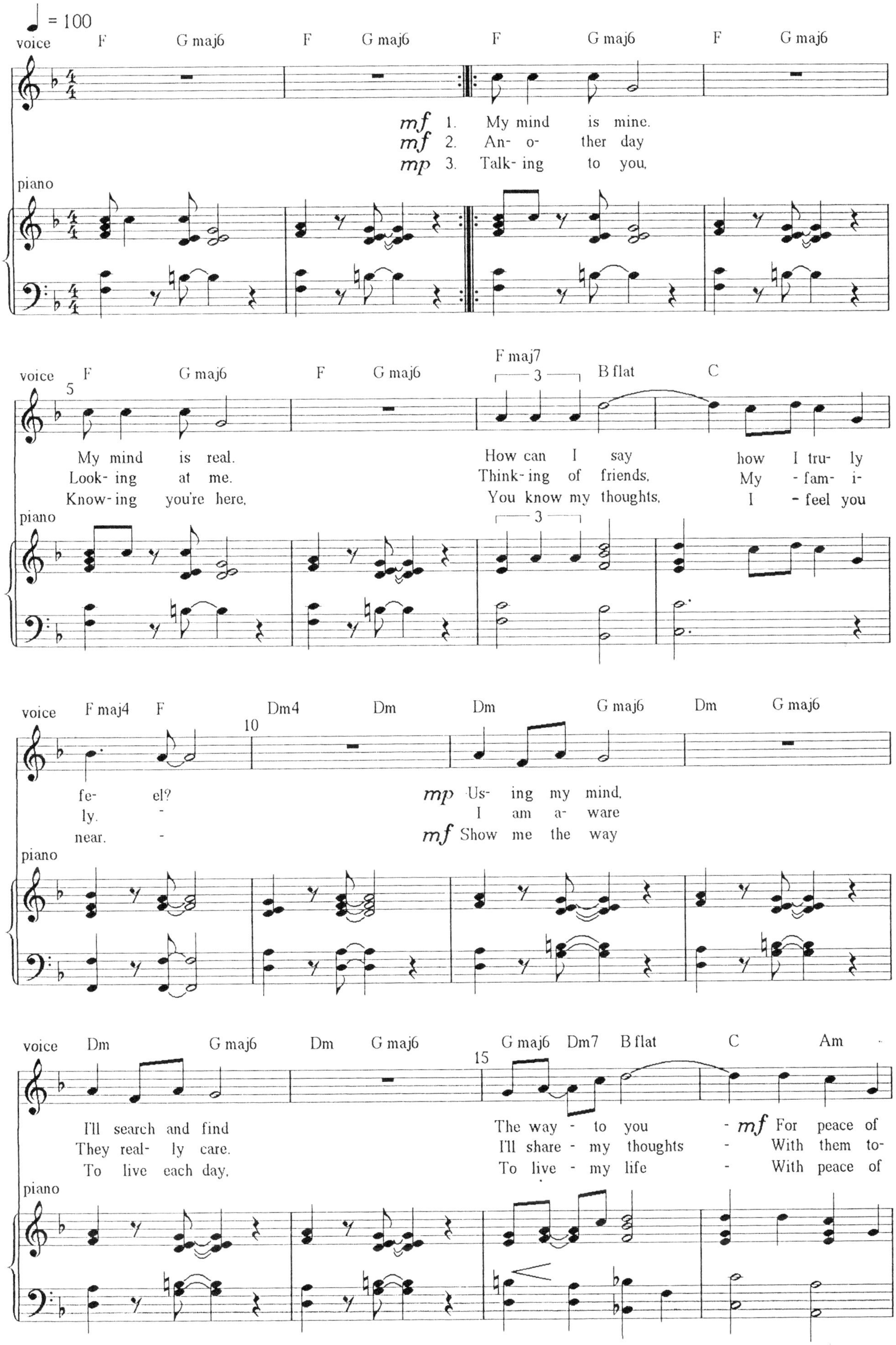

♩ = 100

voice

mf 1. My mind is mine.
mf 2. An- o- ther day
mp 3. Talk- ing to you,

piano

voice

My mind is real. How can I say how I tru- ly
Look- ing at me. Think- ing of friends, My - fam- i-
Know- ing you're here, You know my thoughts, I - feel you

piano

voice

fe- el? *mp* Us- ing my mind,
ly. - I am a- ware
near. - *mf* Show me the way

piano

voice

I'll search and find The way - to you - *mf* For peace of
They real- ly care. I'll share - my thoughts - With them to-
To live each day, To live - my life - With peace of

piano

Topic Songs

1

My mind – Song words

Verse 1 *mf* My mind is mine.
My mind is real.
How can I say
How I truly feel?

mp Using my mind,
I'll search and find

cresc. The way to you

mf For peace of mind,
For peace of mind.

Verse 2 *mf* Another day
Looking at me.
Thinking of friends,
My family.
I am aware
They really care.
I'll share my thoughts
With them today,
With them today.

Verse 3 *mp* Talking to you,
Knowing you're here,
You know my thoughts,
I feel you near.

mf Show me the way
To live each day,
To live my life
With peace of mind,
With peace of mind,
True, true peace of mind.

Topic Songs

3

LET'S CELEBRATE

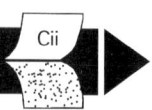

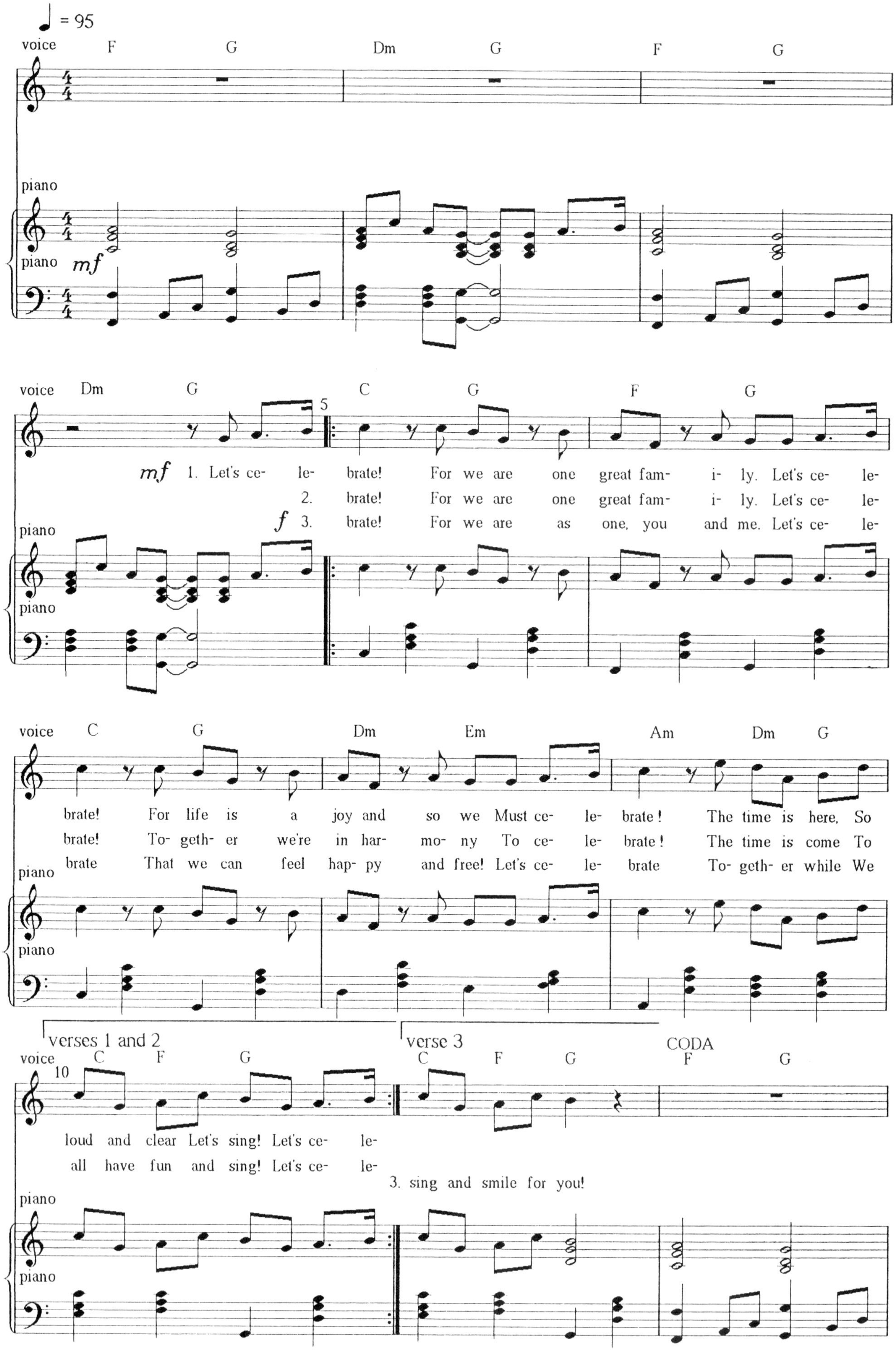

♩ = 95

1. Let's ce- le- brate! For we are one great fam- i- ly. Let's ce- le-
2. brate! For we are one great fam- i- ly. Let's ce- le-
3. brate! For we are as one, you and me. Let's ce- le-

brate! For life is a joy and so we Must ce- le- brate! The time is here, So
brate! To- geth- er we're in har- mo- ny To ce- le- brate! The time is come To
brate That we can feel hap- py and free! Let's ce- le- brate To- geth- er while We

verses 1 and 2

loud and clear Let's sing! Let's ce- le-
all have fun and sing! Let's ce- le-

verse 3

3. sing and smile for you!

CODA

Topic Songs

4

Let's celebrate – Song words

Verse 1   *mf*   Let's celebrate!
For we are one great family.
Let's celebrate!
For life is a joy and so we
Must celebrate!
The time is here,
So loud and clear
Let's sing!

Verse 2   *mf*   Let's celebrate!
For we are one great family.
Let's celebrate!
Together we're in harmony
To celebrate!
The time is come
To all have fun
And sing!

Verse 3   *f*   Let's celebrate!
For we are as one, you and me.
Let's celebrate
That we can feel happy and free!
Let's celebrate
Together while
We sing and smile
For you!

Coda   *p*   Come, let's celebrate!
mp   Come, let's celebrate!
mf   Come, let's celebrate!
f   Let's celebrate!

Topic Songs

COMMUNICATION

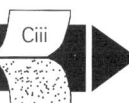

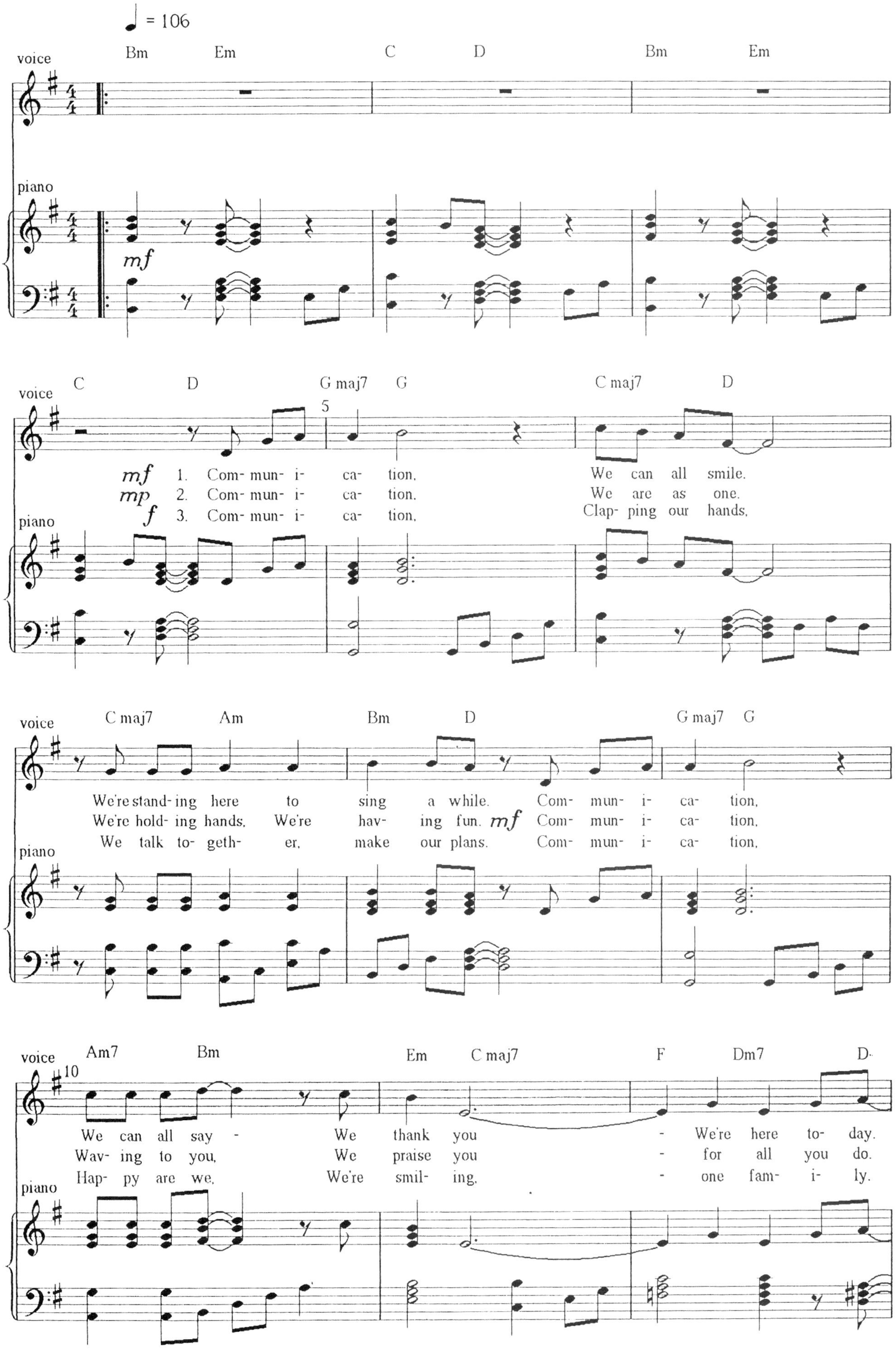

♩ = 106

1. Com-mun-i- ca- tion, We can all smile.
2. Com-mun-i- ca- tion, We are as one.
3. Com-mun-i- ca- tion, Clap- ping our hands,

We're stand-ing here to sing a while. Com- mun- i- ca- tion,
We're hold- ing hands, We're hav- ing fun. Com- mun- i- ca- tion,
We talk to- geth- er, make our plans. Com- mun- i- ca- tion,

We can all say – We thank you – We're here to- day.
Wav- ing to you, We praise you – for all you do.
Hap- py are we. We're smil- ing. – one fam- i- ly.

7

Topic Songs

Communication – Song words

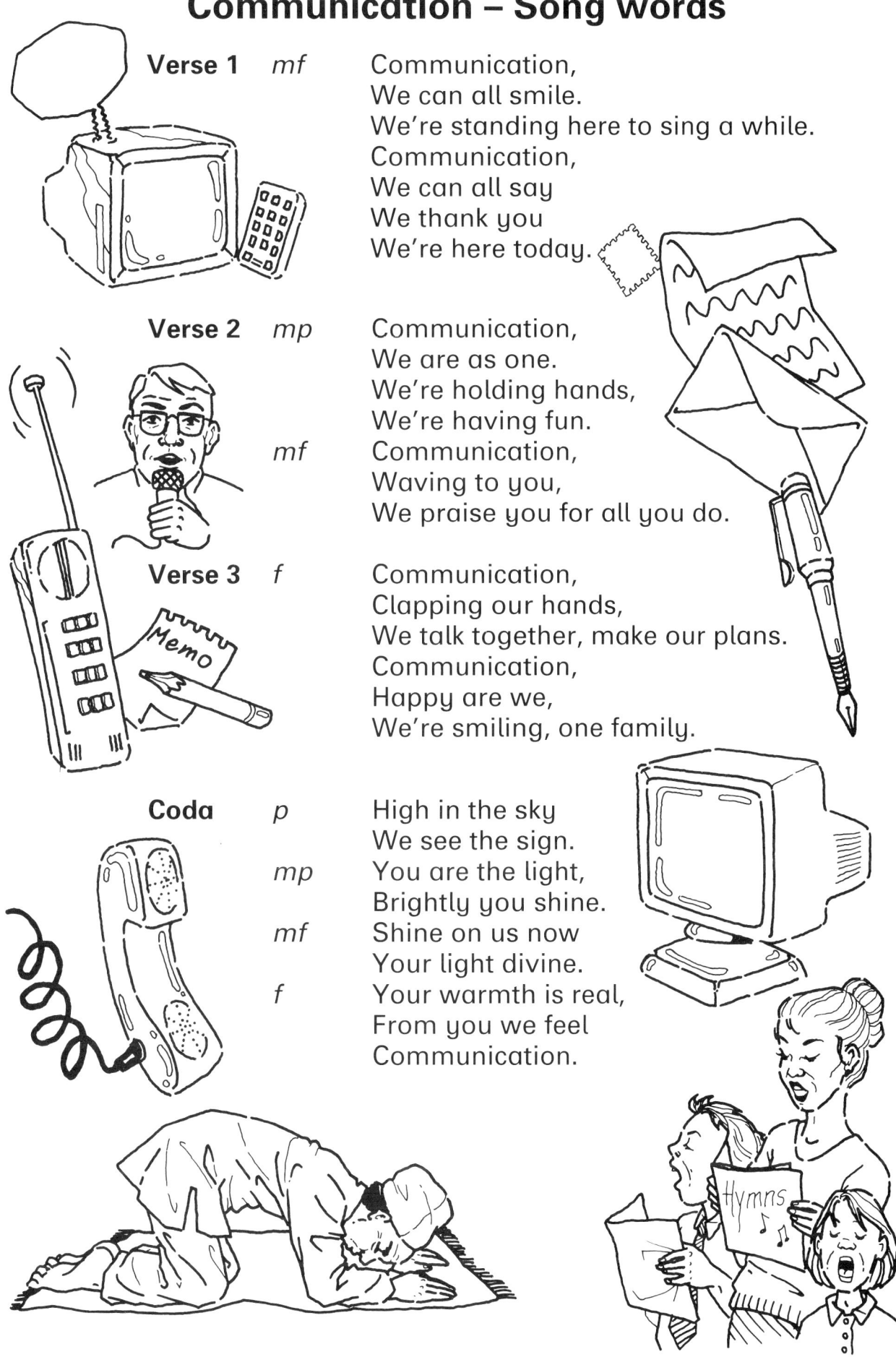

Verse 1 *mf*
Communication,
We can all smile.
We're standing here to sing a while.
Communication,
We can all say
We thank you
We're here today.

Verse 2 *mp*
Communication,
We are as one.
We're holding hands,
We're having fun.
mf
Communication,
Waving to you,
We praise you for all you do.

Verse 3 *f*
Communication,
Clapping our hands,
We talk together, make our plans.
Communication,
Happy are we,
We're smiling, one family.

Coda *p*
High in the sky
We see the sign.
mp
You are the light,
Brightly you shine.
mf
Shine on us now
Your light divine.
f
Your warmth is real,
From you we feel
Communication.

YOU ARE THE ONE

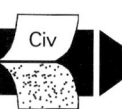

♩. = 57

voice

1. You - are the One, - The
2. You - are the One, - The
3. You - are the One - Who

Giv- er of life - to me. - You - are the One - Whose
light - that shows - the way. - You - are the One - Who
gives me a feel- ing sub- lime. - You - are the One - I'll

love - has set - me free. - You - are - the
guides - me e- ve- ry day. - You - are - the
love 'til the end of all time. - You - are - the

One who turns night - to day. - You - are - the
One - who takes - my hand, - You - are - the
One who is with me al- ways, You - are - the

Topic Songs

10

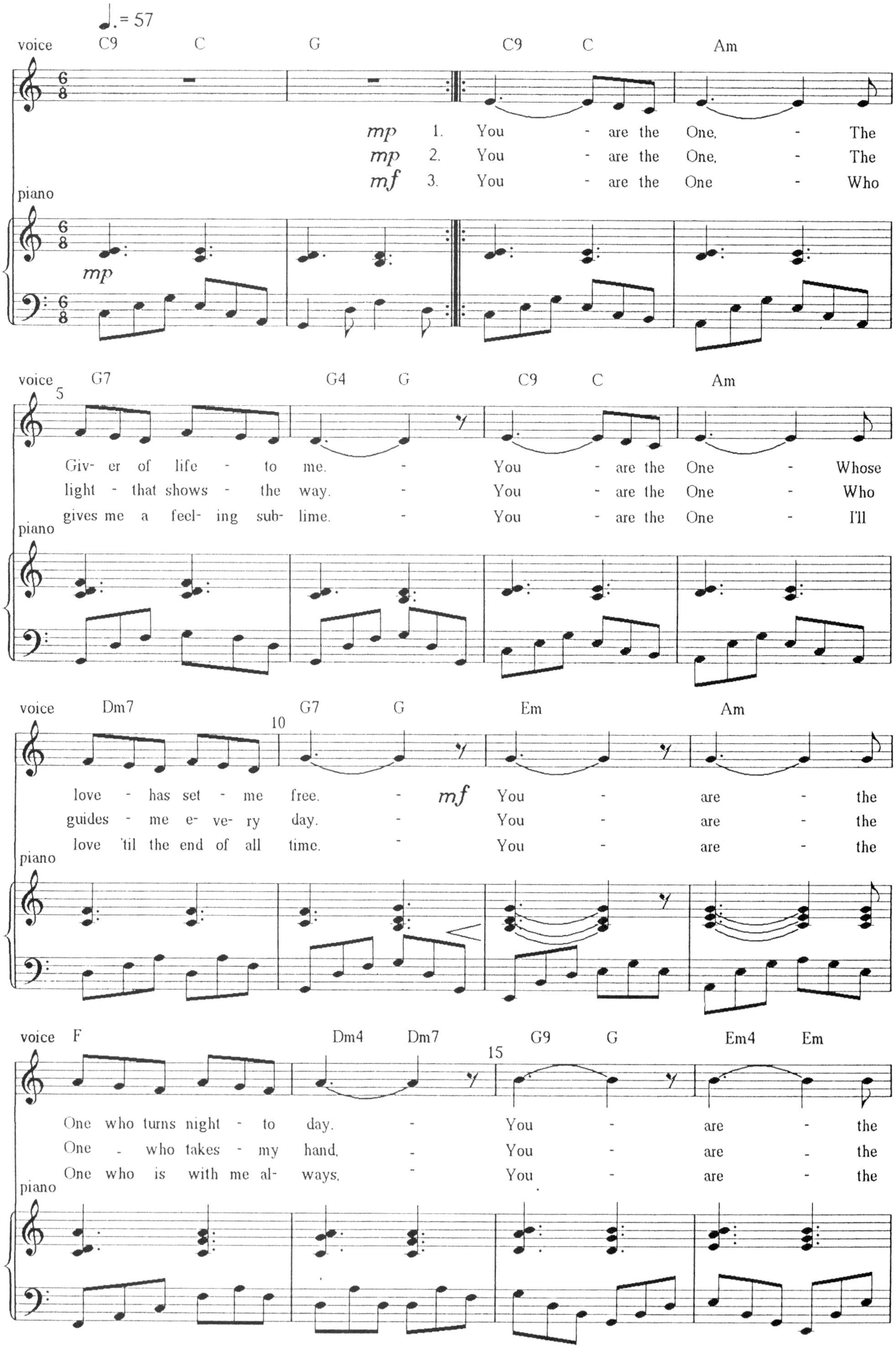

You are the One – Song words

Verse 1   *mp*   You are the One,
                      The Giver of life to me.
                      You are the One
                      Whose love has set me free.
          mf   You are the One who turns night to day.
                      You are the One who sends fear away.

Verse 2   *mp*   You are the One,
                      The light that shows the way.
                      You are the One
                      Who guides me every day.
                      You are the One who takes my hand,
                      You are the One who understands.

Verse 3   *mf*   You are the One
                      Who gives me a feeling sublime.
                      You are the One
                      I'll love 'til the end of all time.
          cresc. You are the One who is with me always,
          f   You are the One who I shower with praise.

Coda   *mf*   You are,
          mp   You are,
          p   You are
                      The One.

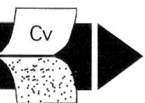

I HAVE FAITH

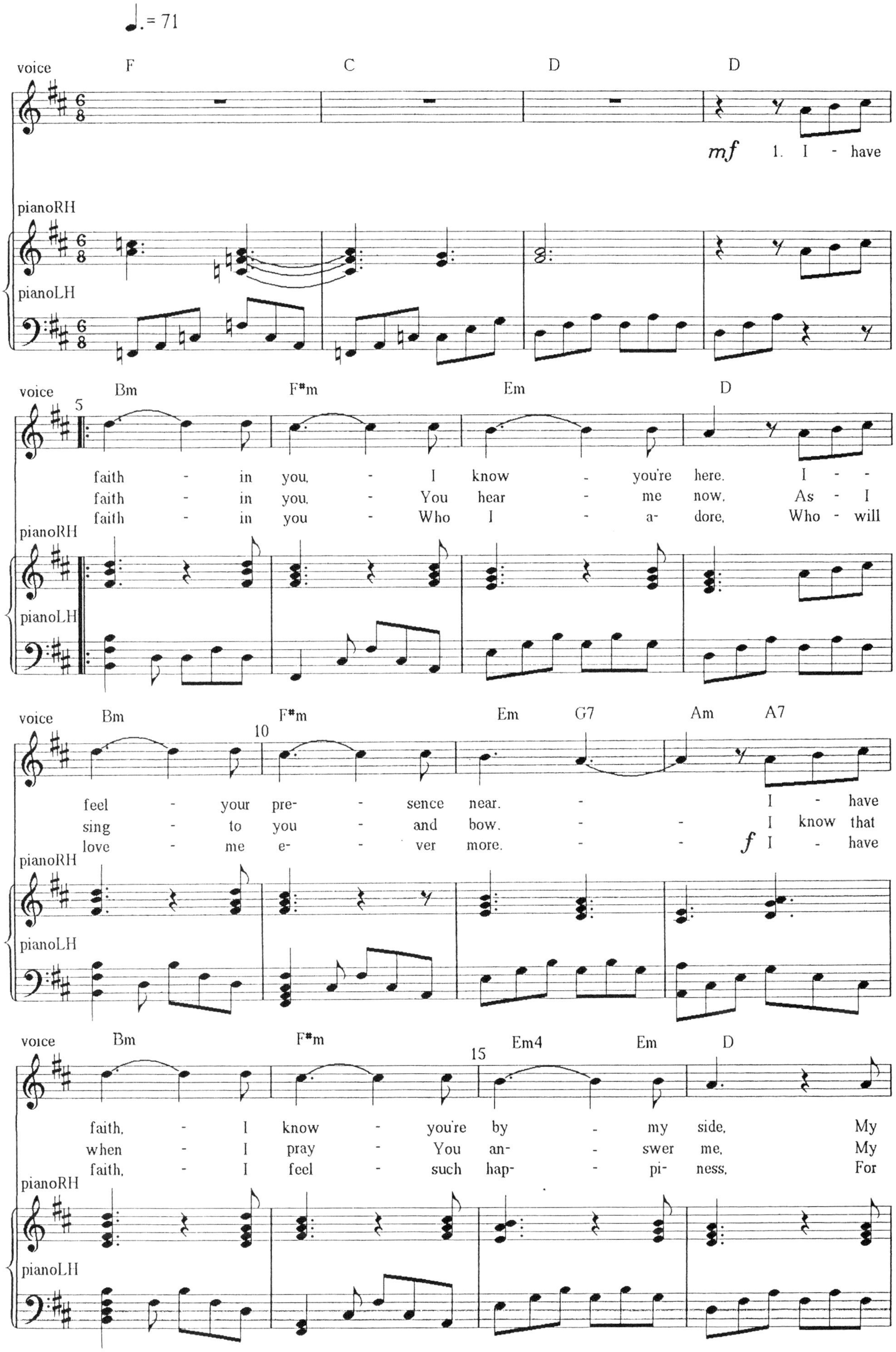

♩.= 71

voice

mf 1. I - have

faith - in you, - I know - you're here. I - -
faith - in you, - You hear - me now. As - I
faith - in you - Who I a- dore, Who - will

feel - your pre- - sence near. - - I - have
sing - to you - and bow. - - I know that
love - me e- - ver more. - - **f** I - have

faith, - I know - you're by - my side, My
when - I pray - You an- - swer me, My
faith, - I feel - such hap- - pi- ness, For

13

Topic Songs

I have faith – Song words

Verse 1 *mf* I have faith in you,
I know you're here.
I feel your presence near.
I have faith,
I know you're by my side,
My friend and my guide.

Verse 2 *mp* I have faith in you,
You hear me now,
As I sing to you and bow.
I know that when I pray
You answer me,
My spirit is free.

Verse 3 *mf* I have faith in you
Who I adore,
Who will love me evermore.
f I have faith,
I feel such happiness,
For I know I'm blessed.
I know,
I know I'm blessed.

Topic Songs

SACRED LIVES

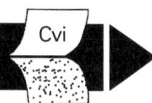

♩. = 45

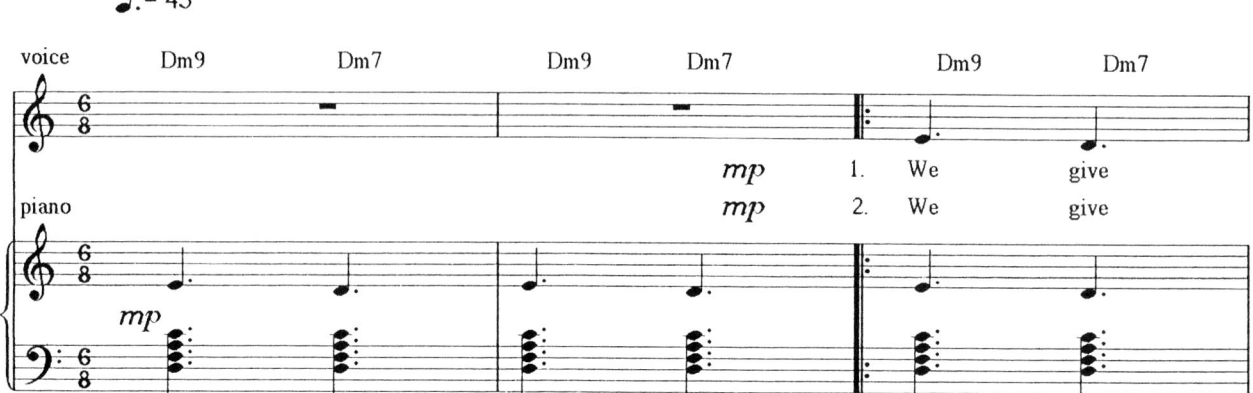

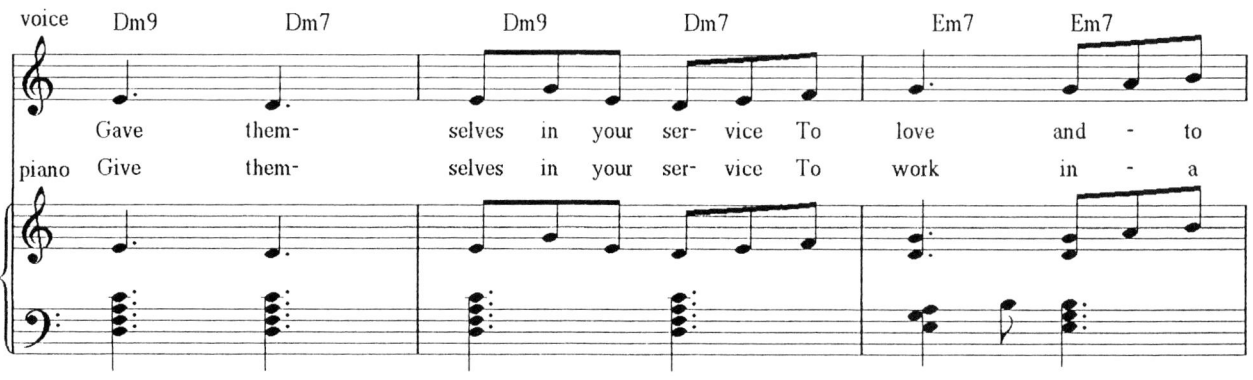

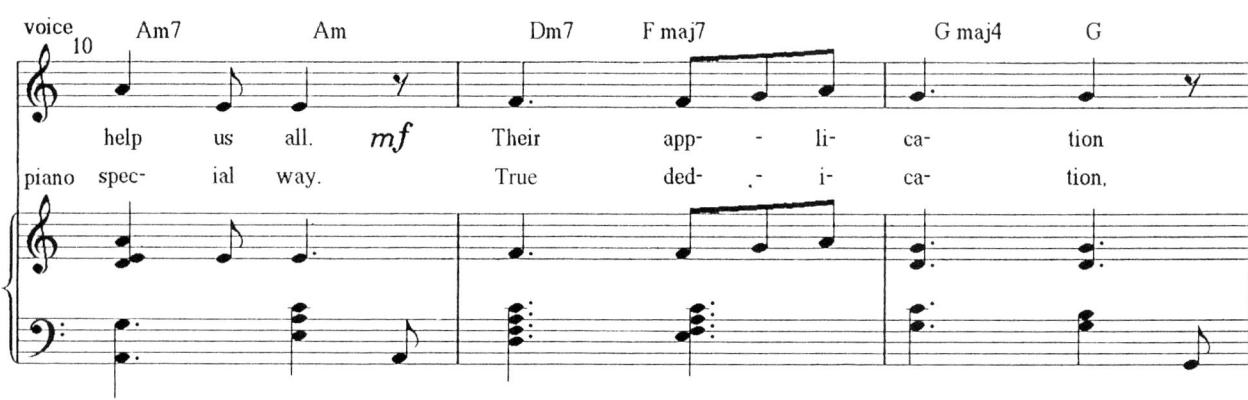

16

Sacred lives – Song words

Verse 1   *mp*   We give thanks for the people
Who answered the call.
Gave themselves in your service
To love and to help us all.

             mf   Their application
Brought great salvation
We give thanks for them all.

Verse 2   *mp*   We give thanks for the people
Who help us today.
Give themselves in your service
To work in a special way.
True dedication,

             mf   Our inspiration.
We give thanks for their lives,
Sacred lives.

Topic Songs

THE GOLDEN RAY

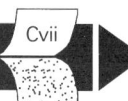

♩ = 100

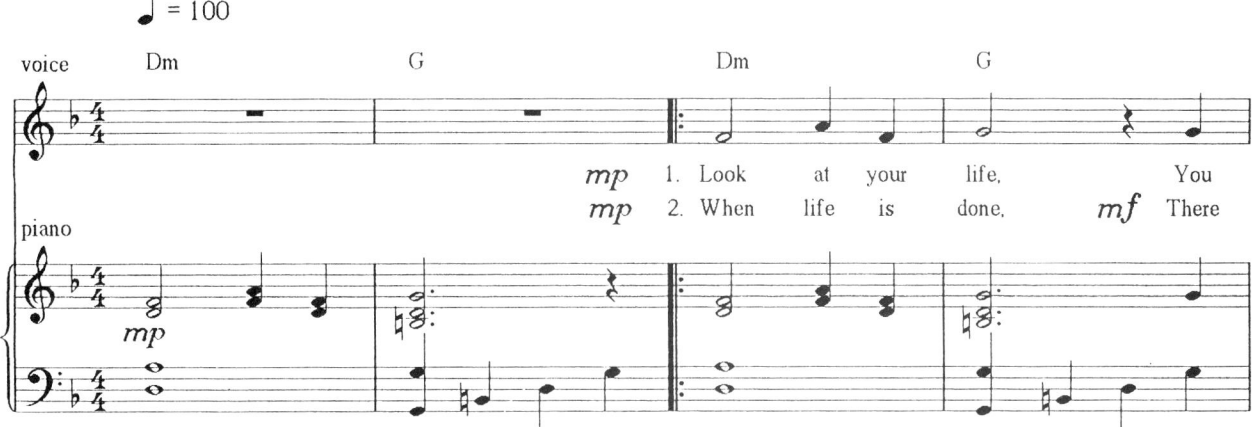

voice | Dm | G | Dm | G

mp 1. Look at your life, You
mp 2. When life is done, *mf* There

voice | Dm | G | C | Am

want to find suc- cess. You're search- ing for a
is the Gold- en Ray. This rad- iant beam Leads

voice | Dm | G | Dm | G

life of hap- pi- ness. Think of your- self Be-
to e- ter- nal day. *mp* When loved ones rest, The

voice | Dm | G | C | Am

yond your earth- ly life. There is a joy To
ones we loved the best. *mf* The Gold- en Ray Has

19

Topic Songs

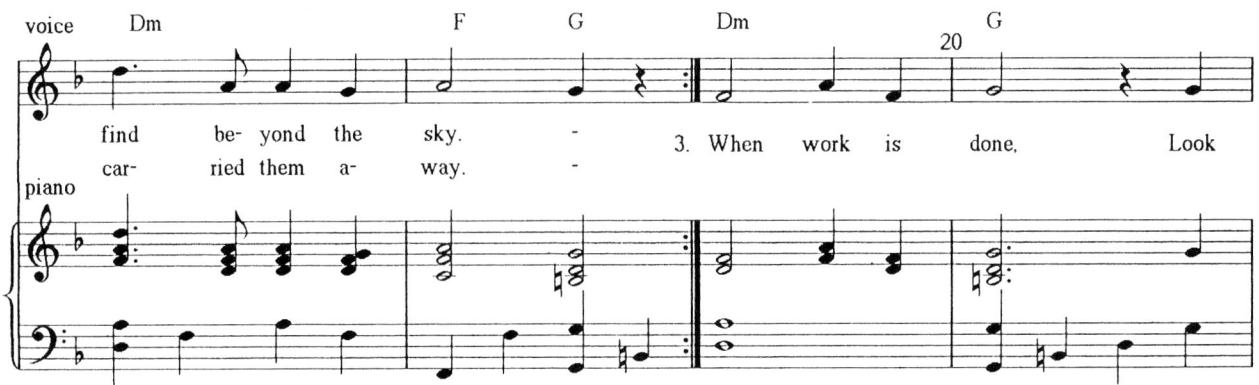

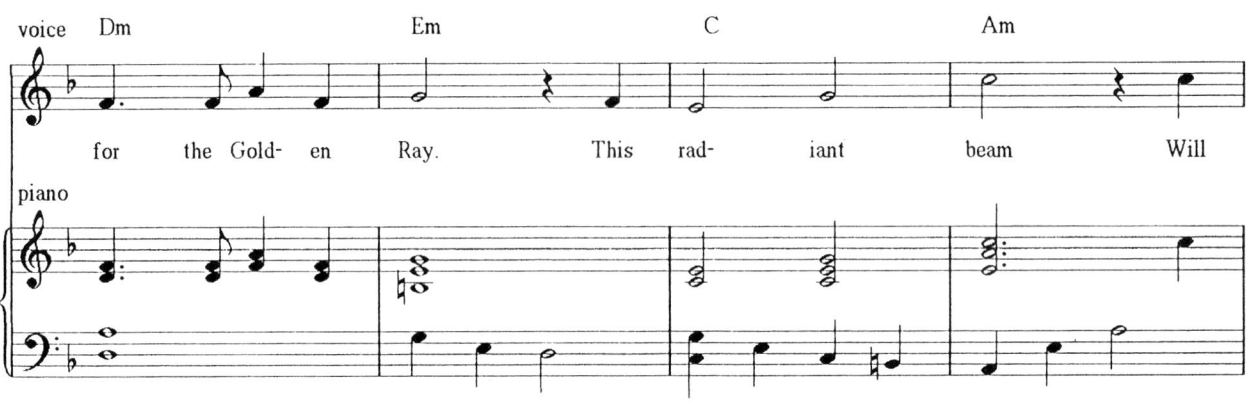

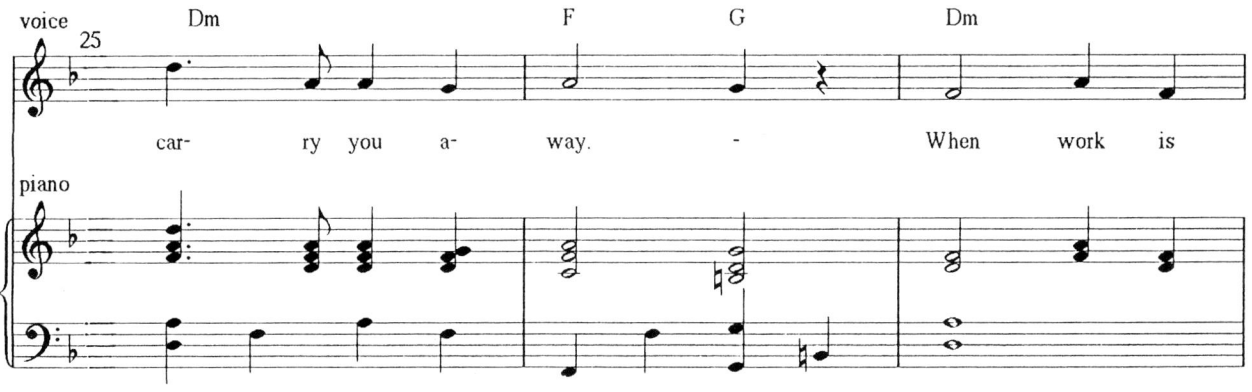

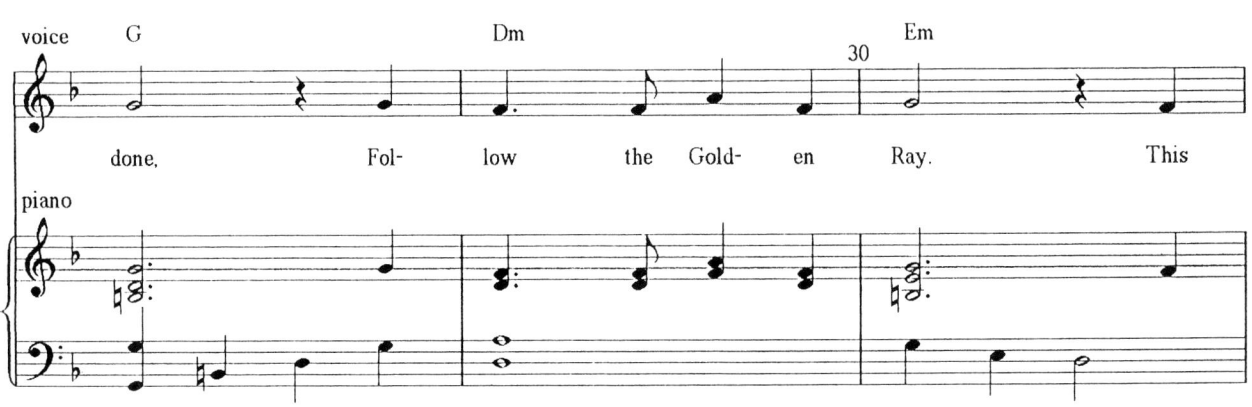

Topic Songs

The Golden Ray – Song words

Verse 1   *mp*   Look at your life,
You want to find success.
You're searching for
A life of happiness.
Think of yourself
Beyond your earthly life.
There is a joy
To find beyond the sky.

Verse 2   *mp*   When life is done,
           mf   There is the Golden Ray.
This radiant beam
Leads to eternal day.
           mp   When loved ones rest,
The ones we loved the best.
           mf   The Golden Ray
Has carried them away.

Verse 3   *mp*   When work is done,
Look for the Golden Ray.
           mf   This radiant beam
Will carry you away.
When work is done,
Follow the Golden Ray.
This radiant beam
Leads to eternal day,
Will lead you
To eternal day.

Topic Songs

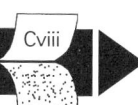

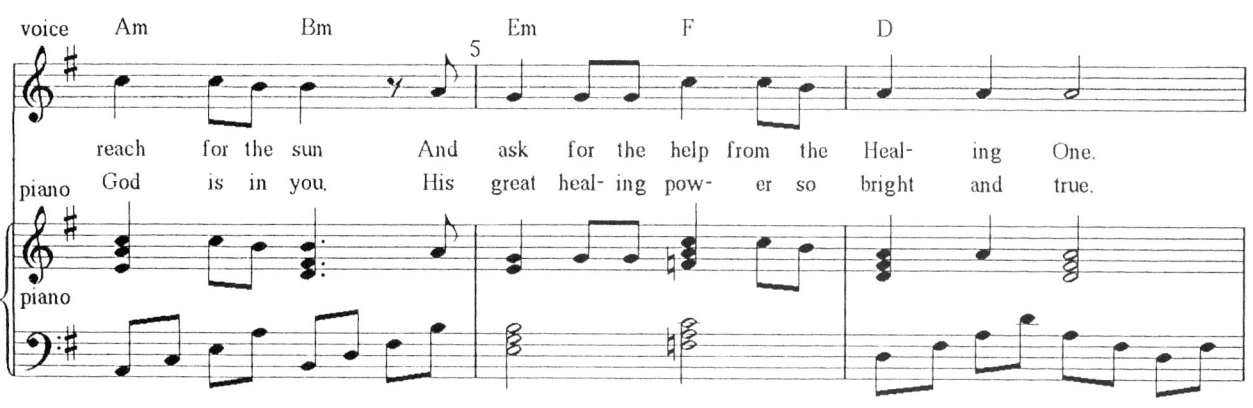

23

Topic Songs

Topic Songs

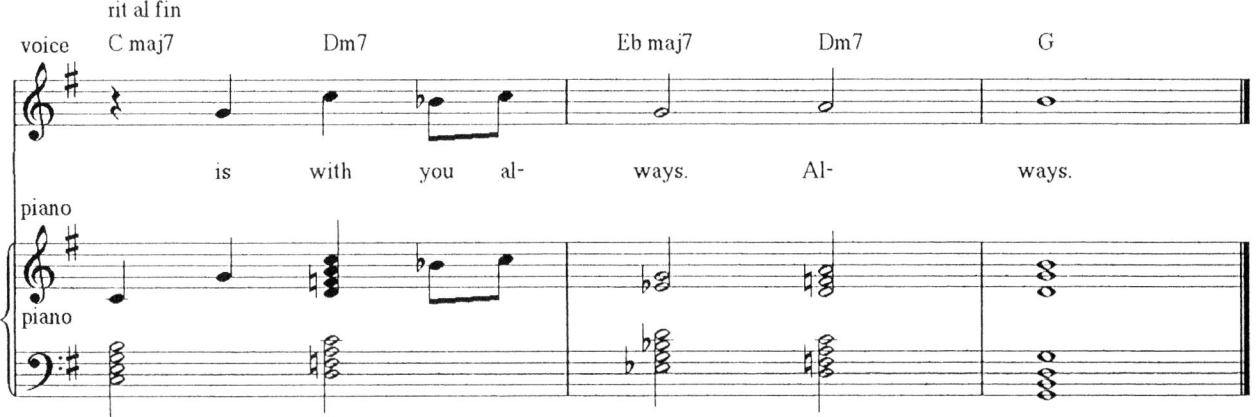

is with you al- ways. Al- ways.

Topic Songs

Rise, rise, rise! – Song words

Verse 1   *mp*   Rise, rise and reach for the sun
And ask for the help from the Healing One.
Rise, rise through night and day,
The healing light will show us the way.

Chorus   *mf*   Rise, rise, rise!
Rise, rise, rise!

Verse 2   *mf*   Rise, rise, for God is in you,
His great healing power so bright and true.
Rise, rise and seek His pure light,
mp   Freed from the dark, the shadows of night.

Chorus   *mf*   Rise, rise, rise!
Rise, rise, rise!

Verse 3   *mp*   Rise, rise, the glow will grow,
mf   The great healing flame will burn and show
f   God's love lights up the way,
His healing light is with you always,
His healing light is with you always,
Always.

Topic Songs

OTHER PEOPLE COUNT

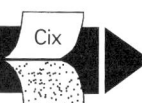

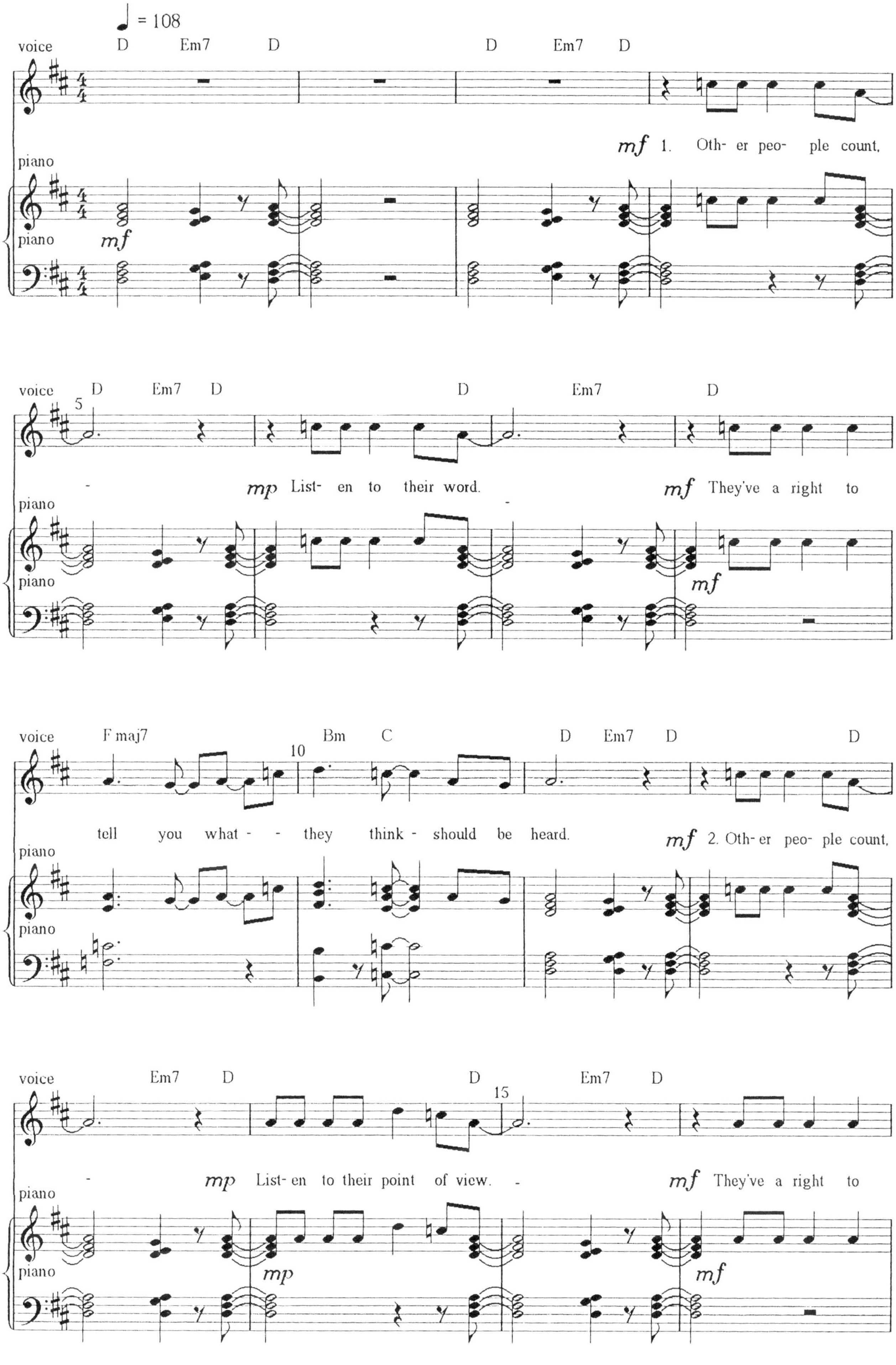

♩ = 108

Verse 1: Oth-er peo-ple count,

mp List-en to their word. mf They've a right to tell you what they think should be heard.

2. Oth-er peo-ple count,

mp List-en to their point of view. mf They've a right to

Topic Songs

Topic Songs

Other people count – Song words

Verse 1 *mf* Other people count,
         mp Listen to their word.
         mf They've a right to tell you
              What they think should be heard.

Verse 2 *mf* Other people count,
         mp Listen to their point of view.
         mf They've a right to tell you
              What they think is true.

Verse 3 *mf* Listen now to someone else,
              Share with them your point of view.
              You can now compare
              What you both think is true.

Verse 4 *mf* Listen to the people now,
              They can speak to you somehow.
              Put across what matters to them,
              And that's how –

Verse 5 *f* Other people count,
              Listen to their word.
              They've a right to tell you
              What they think should be heard.

Verse 6 *f* Other people count,
              Listen to their point of view.
              They've a right to tell you
              What they think is true.

Coda *mf* It's ABC.
              Don't you agree?
         cresc. For you and me
              It's plain to see
         f Other people count.
              Other people count,
              Other people count.

Topic Songs

31

COPYMASTERS
1–90

First name search

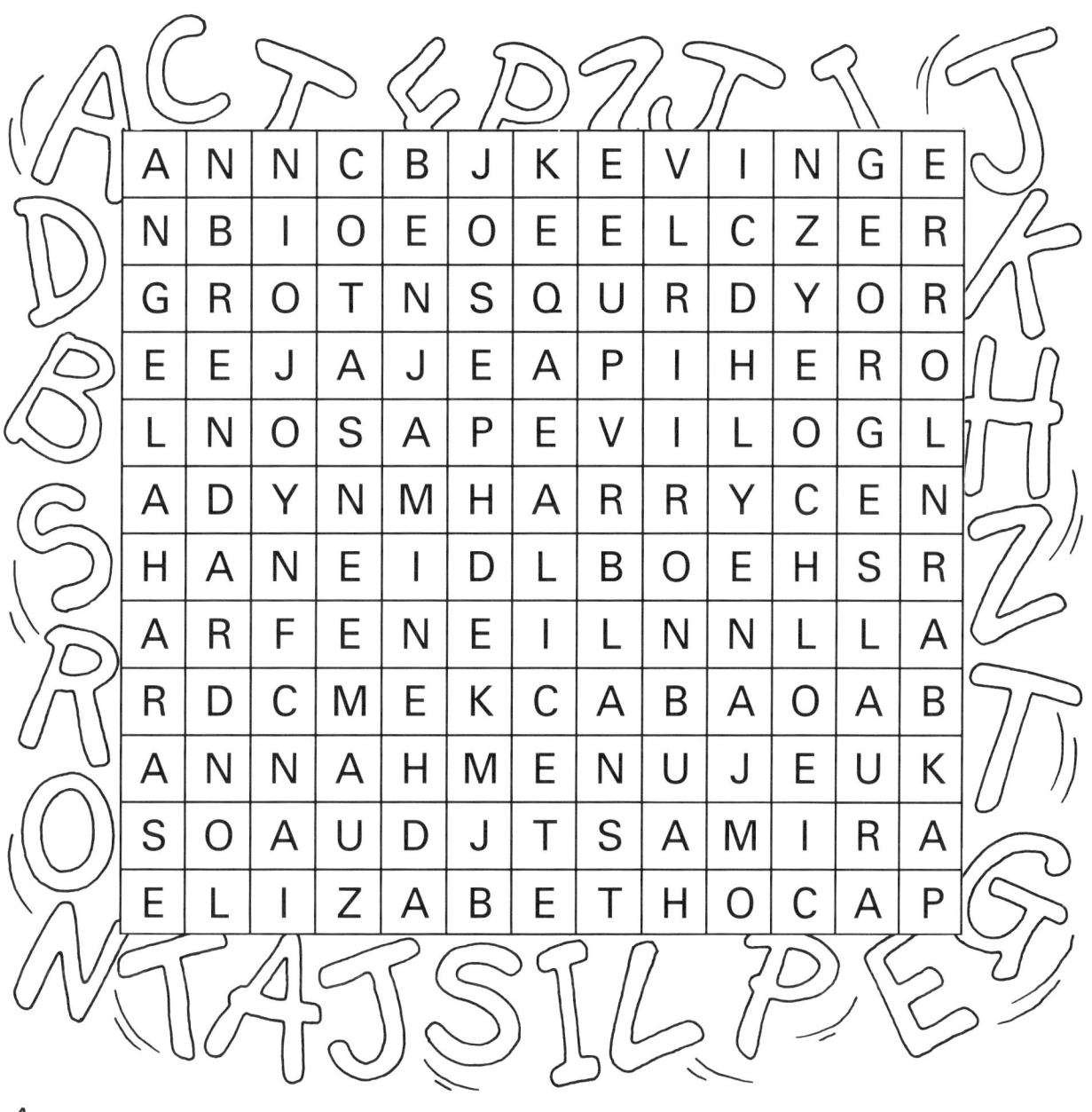

A	N	N	C	B	J	K	E	V	I	N	G	E
N	B	I	O	E	O	E	E	L	C	Z	E	R
G	R	O	T	N	S	Q	U	R	D	Y	O	R
E	E	J	A	J	E	A	P	I	H	E	R	O
L	N	O	S	A	P	E	V	I	L	O	G	L
A	D	Y	N	M	H	A	R	R	Y	C	E	N
H	A	N	E	I	D	L	B	O	E	H	S	R
A	R	F	E	N	E	I	L	N	N	L	L	A
R	D	C	M	E	K	C	A	B	A	O	A	B
A	N	N	A	H	M	E	N	U	J	E	U	K
S	O	A	U	D	J	T	S	A	M	I	R	A
E	L	I	Z	A	B	E	T	H	O	C	A	P

Ann   Akbar   Anna   Benjamin   Alice   David   Brenda

Tasneem   Elizabeth   George   Angela   Bikhu

       Jane   Harry   Neil

                                                              Sarah

Paul Zi Roy   Jean   Ian   Joy   Eric   Chloe   Errol

Joseph June Kevin   Samira   Lo   Laura   Lee   Olive   Leo

Welcome cards

How I welcome a new boy or girl to my street ...

How I welcome a new boy or girl to my class ...

How I would feel in these situations ...

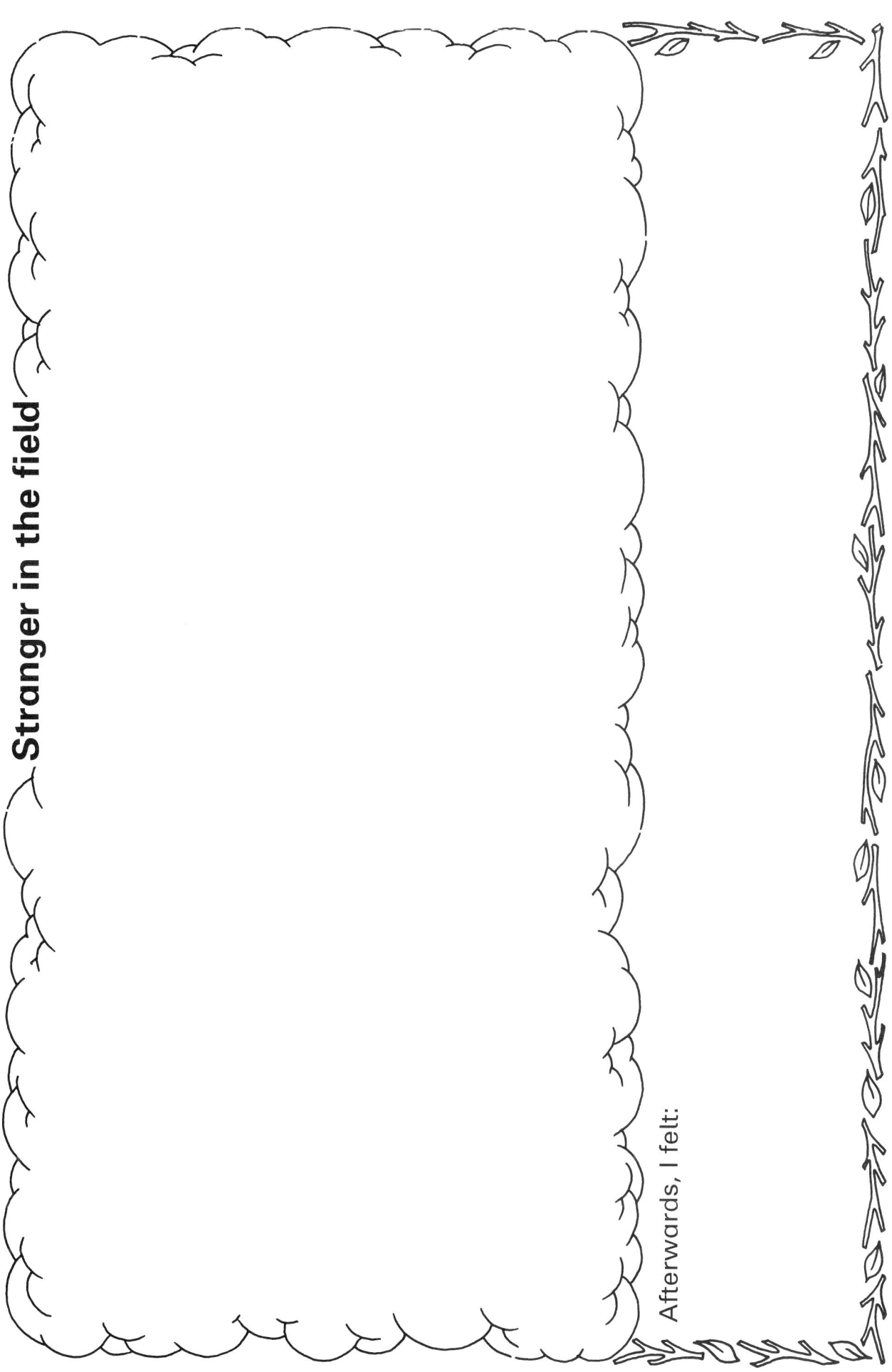

Stranger in the field

Afterwards, I felt:

✔ **My wonderful mind C3**

The human brain

personality
(frontal lobe)

grey matter

sensations
(sensory cortex)

brain stem

brain
(cerebrum)

white matter

balance
(cerebellum)

voluntary movement
(motor cortex)

My wonderful mind C4

States of mind

My wonderful mind C5

What would I do next?

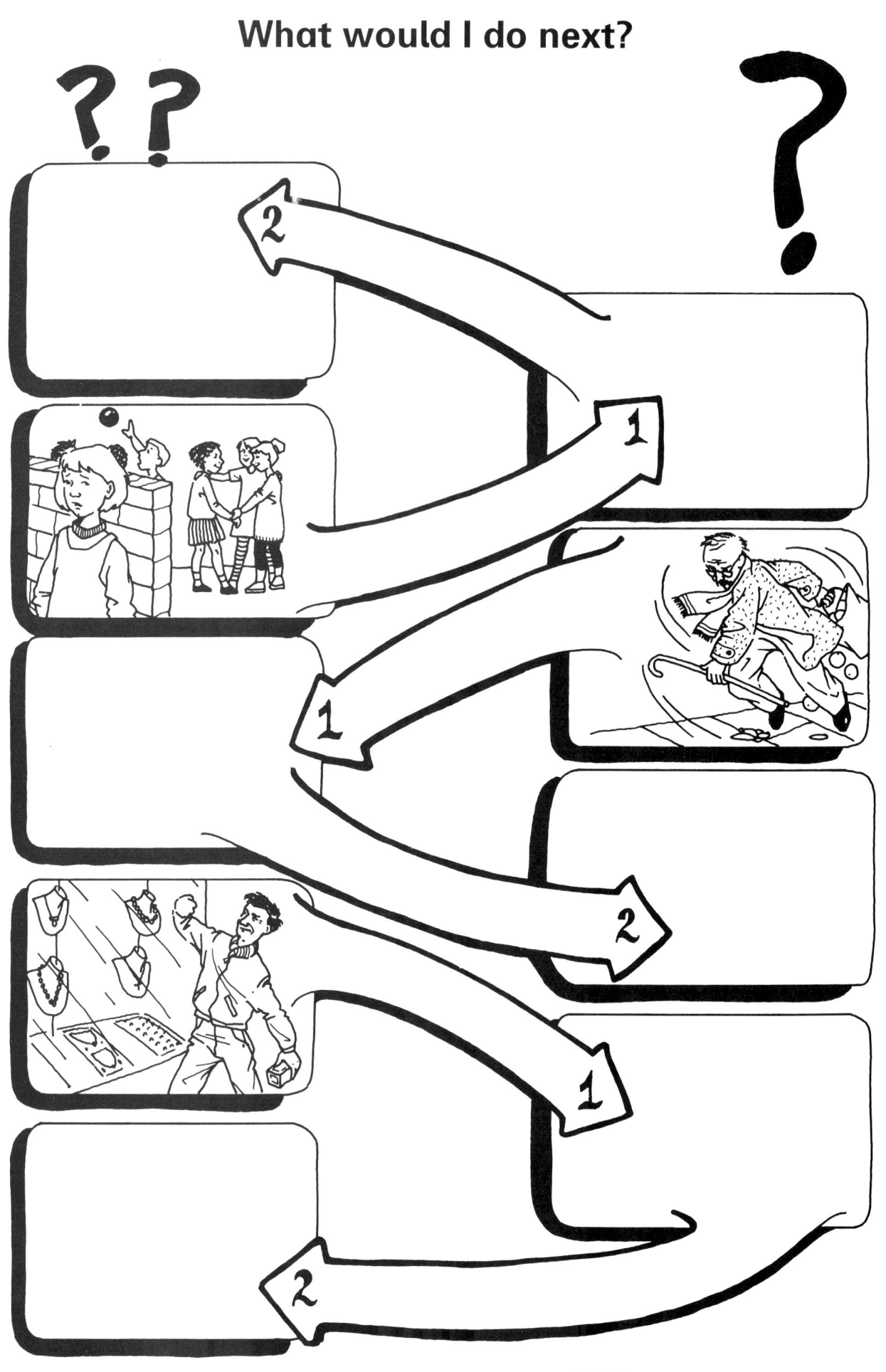

My wonderful mind C6

Kori's flower mobile

My wonderful mind C7

Action and response

Clues

Across
1. Your teacher is _____ if you forget something. (5)
3. You feel _____ when you receive a present. (9)
5. You tidy your bedroom and Mum feels _____. (7)
7. You share your sweets and your friend feels _____. (4)
9. Mum or Dad hugs you and you feel _____. (5)

Down
2. Your friend moves away and you feel _____. (3)
4. You do a good deed and you feel _____. (5)
6. If you hurt someone's feelings they can feel _____. (7)
8. You do something wrong and you feel _____. (7)

My wonderful mind C8

Choices

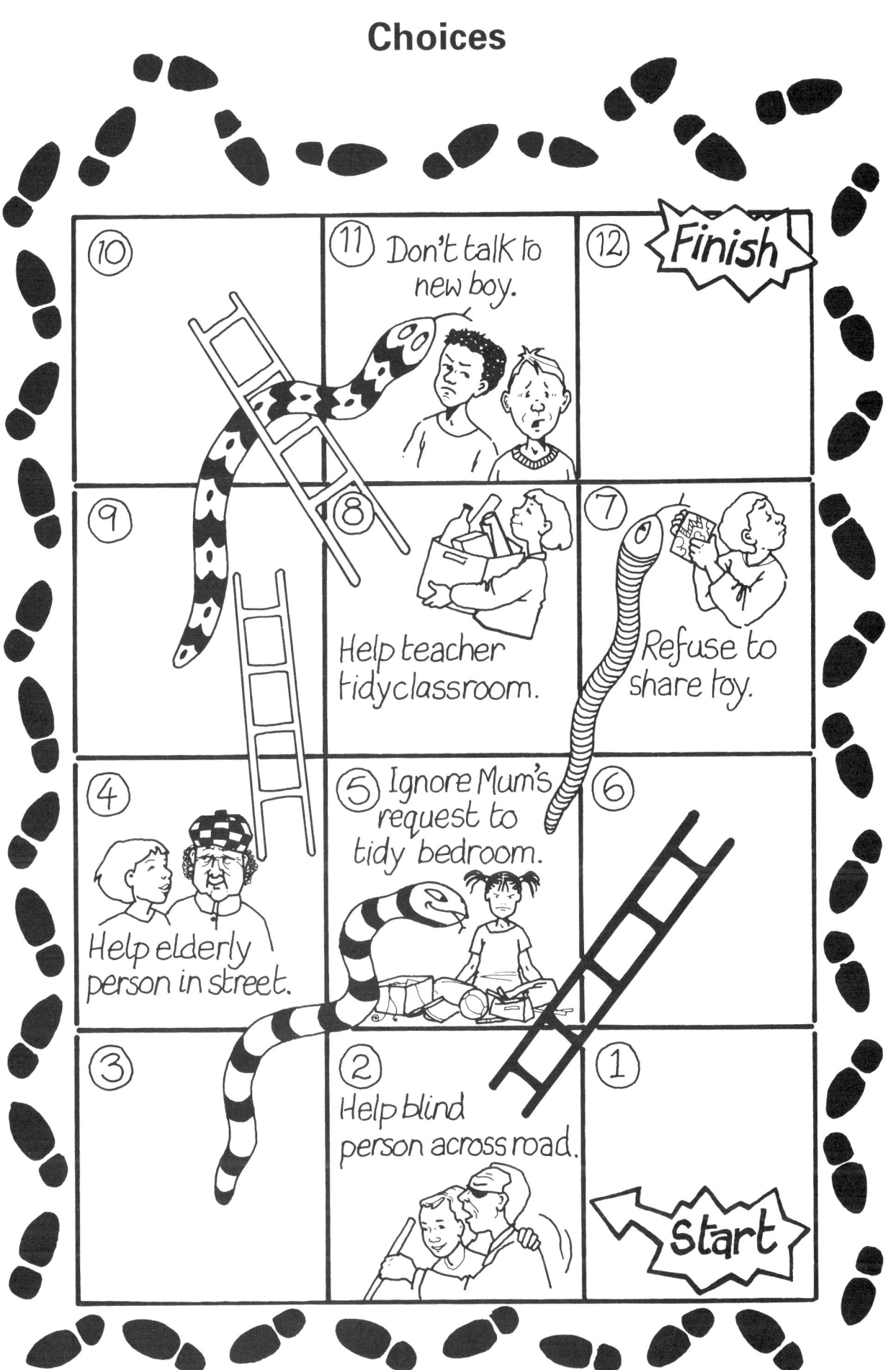

Weekly help index

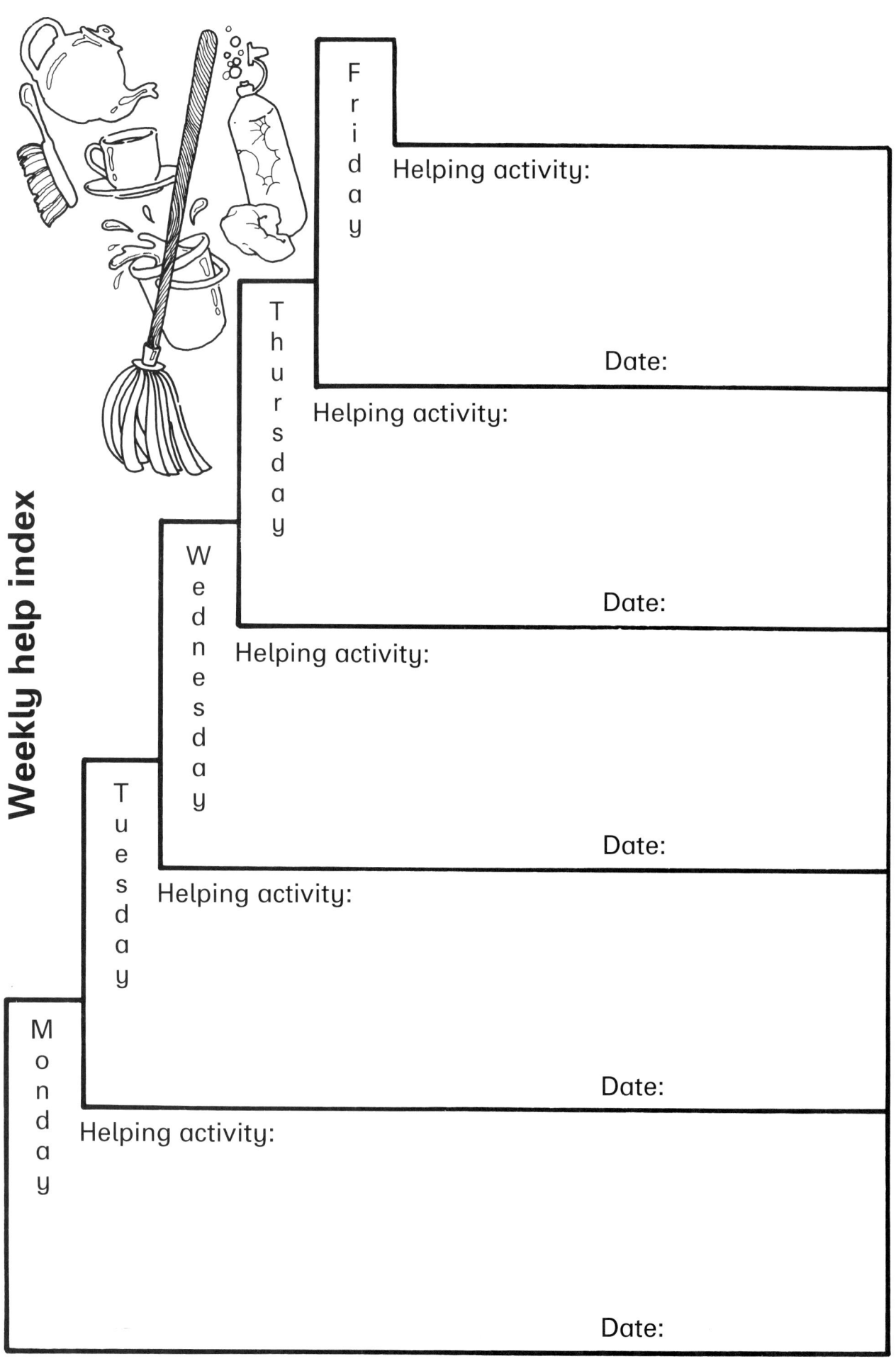

Friday

Helping activity:

Date:

Thursday

Helping activity:

Date:

Wednesday

Helping activity:

Date:

Tuesday

Helping activity:

Date:

Monday

Helping activity:

Date:

42

Easter scroll 1

Let's celebrate C11

Easter scroll 2

44

Easter scroll 3

On Palm Sunday, Jesus rode into Jerusalem on a donkey. Crowds cheered. They shouted 'Hosanna!' and waved palms.

The next day Jesus visited the temple and knocked over the merchants' goods stalls, shouting, 'My house is a house of prayer'.

Judas, one of Jesus' disciples, told Jesus' enemies where they could find him to arrest him. He was paid 30 silver coins.

In an upper room, Jesus shared his last meal with his disciples. He broke bread and said, 'This is my body which will be broken for you.' He drank wine and said, 'This is my blood which will be shed for you.'

Judas led the soldiers to the Garden of Gethsemane near the foot of the Mount of Olives. He showed the soldiers who Jesus was with a kiss. Jesus was arrested and led away to be sentenced to death.

Jesus was nailed to a wooden cross and was crucified.

He was placed in a tomb cut from rock and a large stone was rolled in front of the entrance.

On the third morning after he had died Mary Magdalene visited the tomb. She saw two angels who told her Jesus had risen from the dead. She left to tell the others the Good News.

45

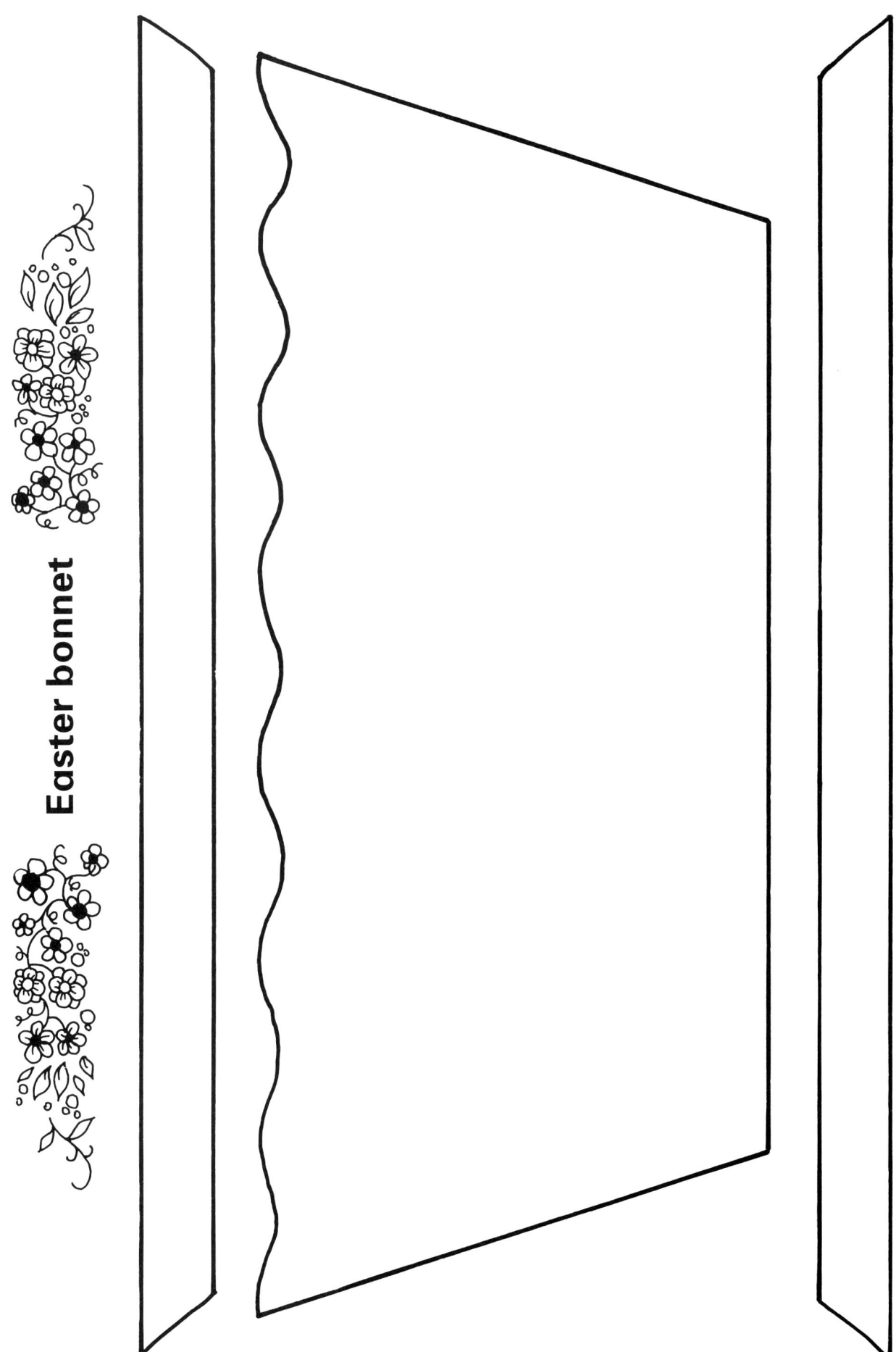

Easter bonnet

Let's celebrate C14

The Sikh uniform

Let's celebrate C15

Celebrating Baisakhi

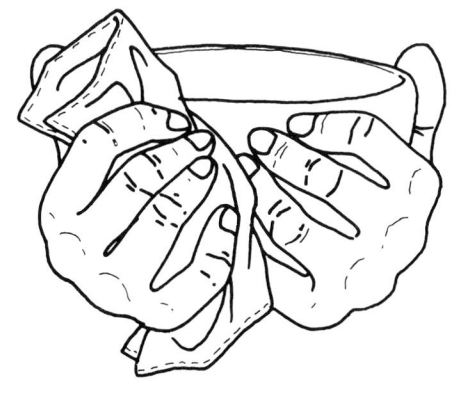

Let's celebrate C16

Holi bonfire blaze

Let's celebrate C17

Om

Let's celebrate C18

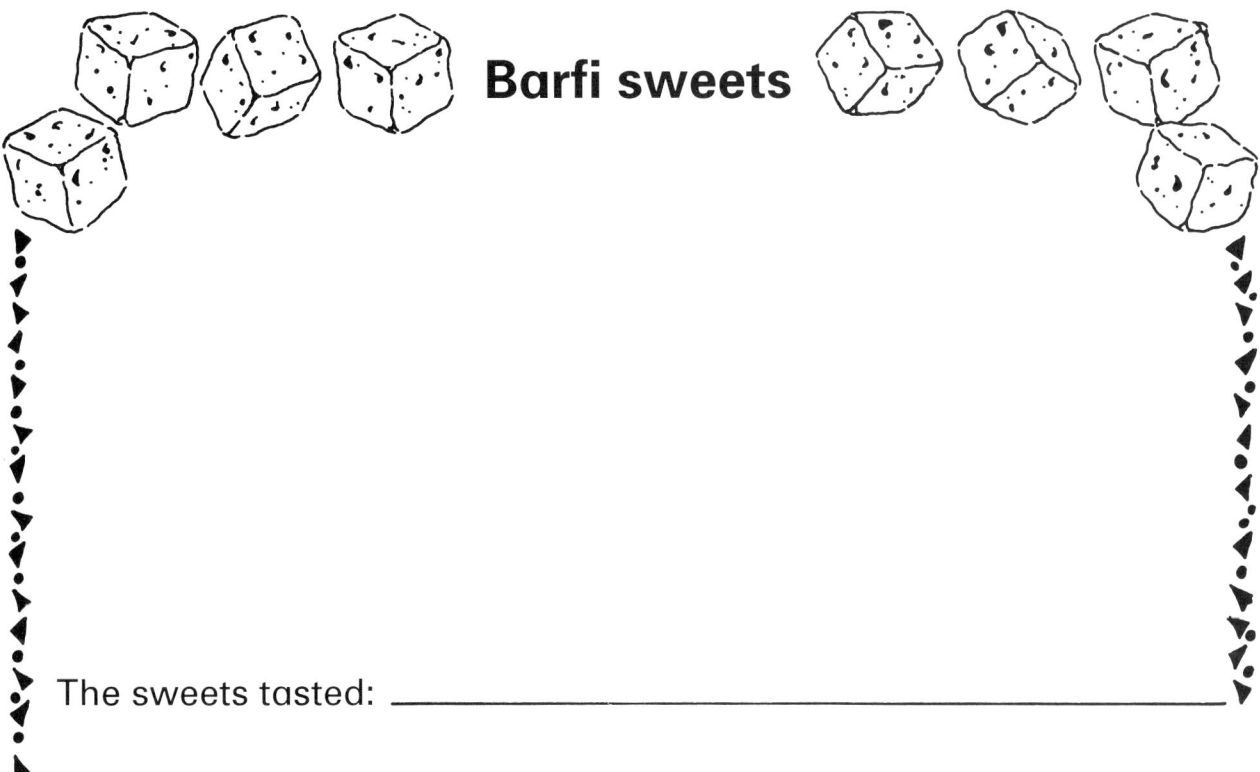

Barfi sweets

The sweets tasted: _____

_____

Ingredients

evaporated milk   4 ozs sugar   8 ozs dried coconut   nuts and cherries

Method

1. Pour large can of _____ into saucepan.
   Place over low heat.
   Stir continuously and add 4 ozs _____.

2. Gradually add _____, stirring thoroughly.

3. Sprinkle _____ and _____ on to the mixture.

4. Pour evenly into a greased tin. Leave to _____ until the
   following day. Cut into cubes and serve.

51

Remembering Holi

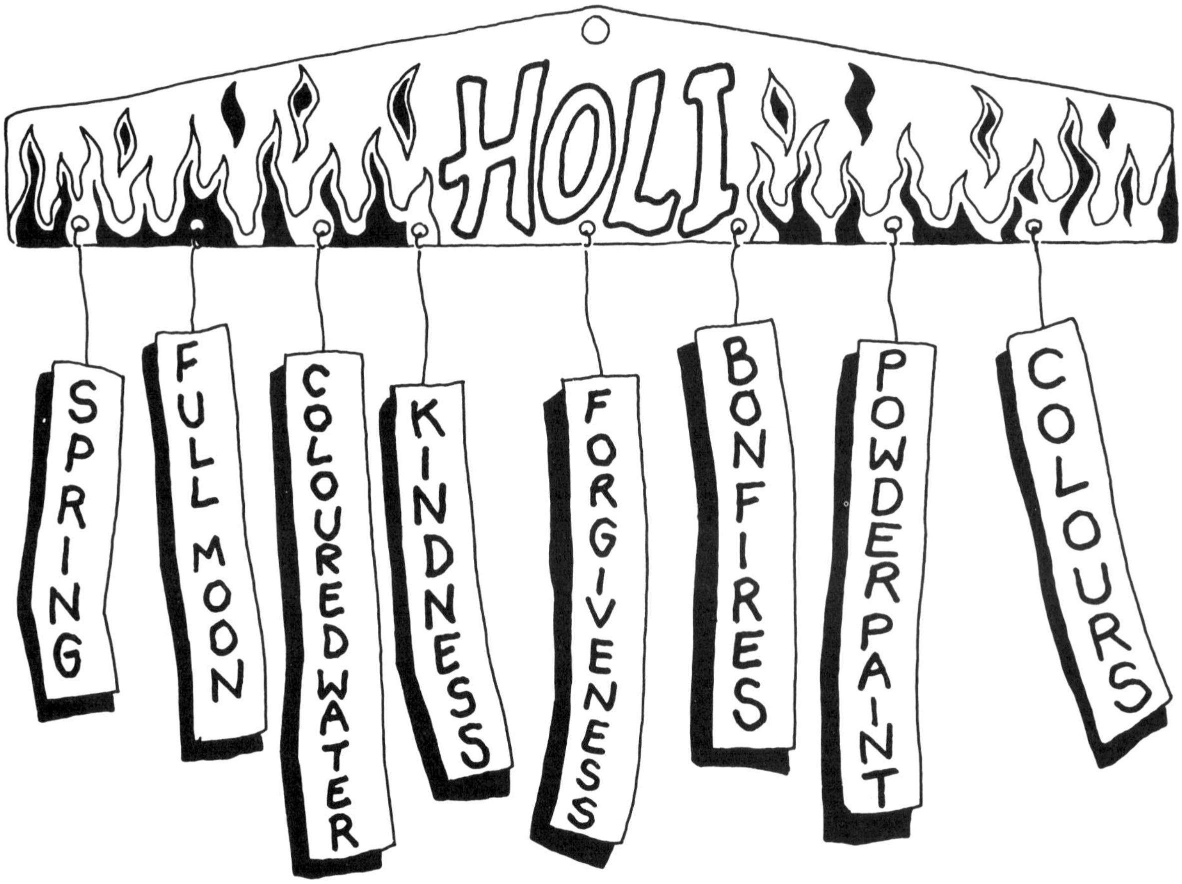

HOLI
SPRING
FULL MOON
COLOUREDWATER
KINDNESS
FORGIVENESS
BONFIRES
POWDERPAINT
COLOURS

Let's celebrate C20

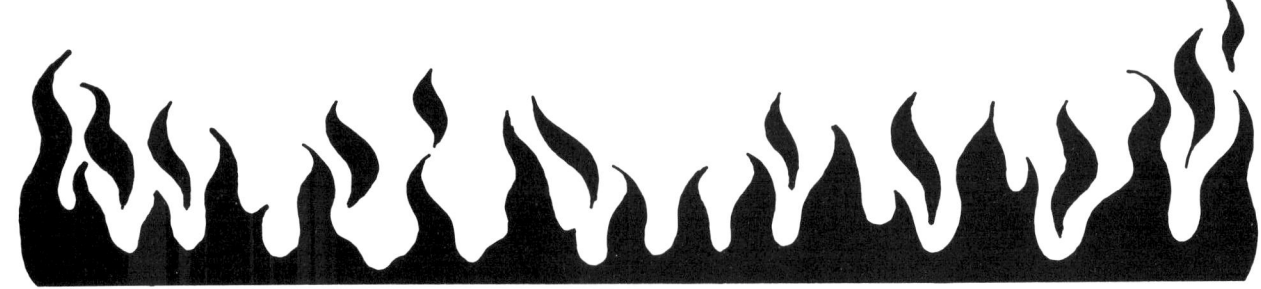

Hand communication

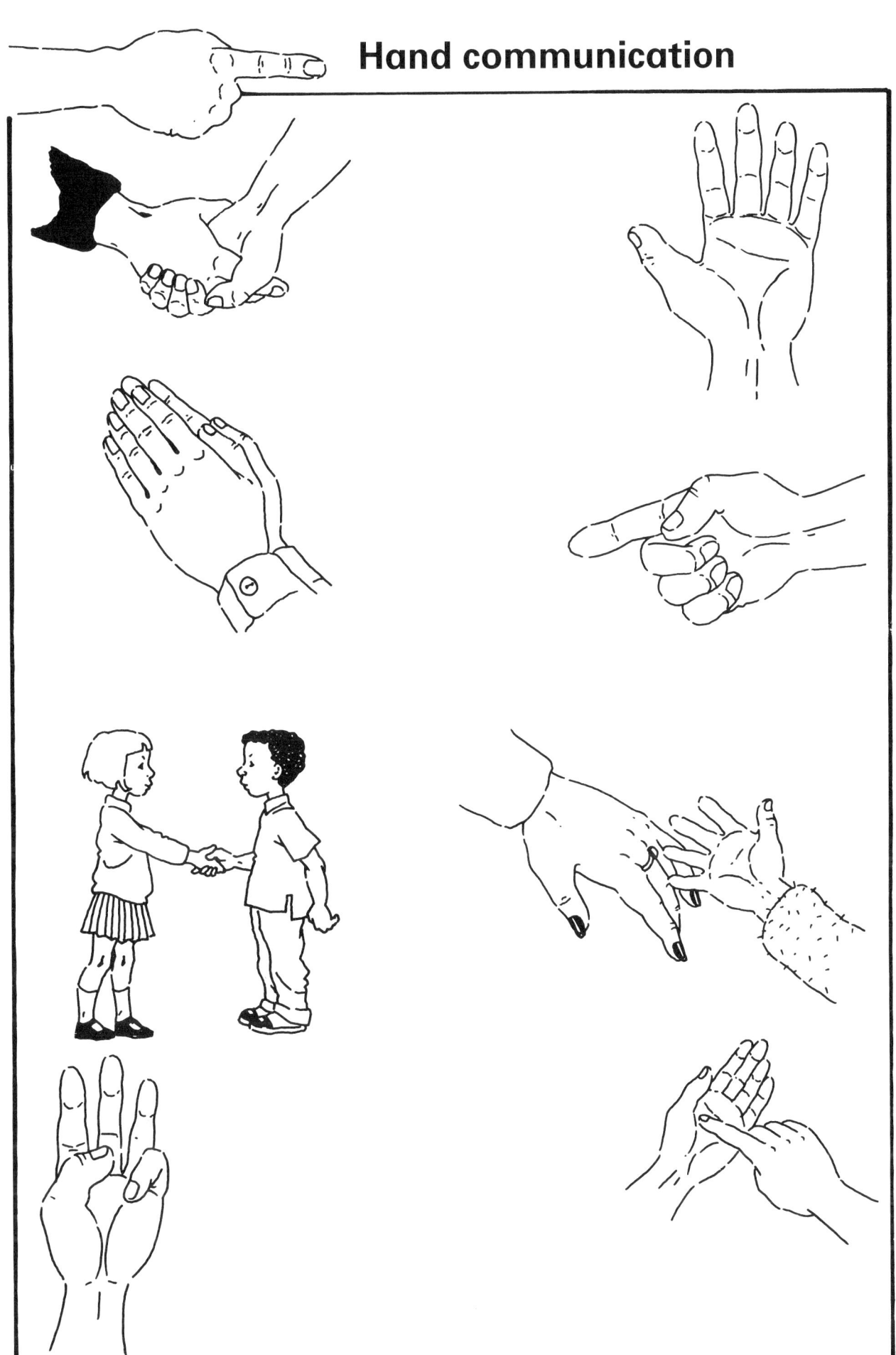

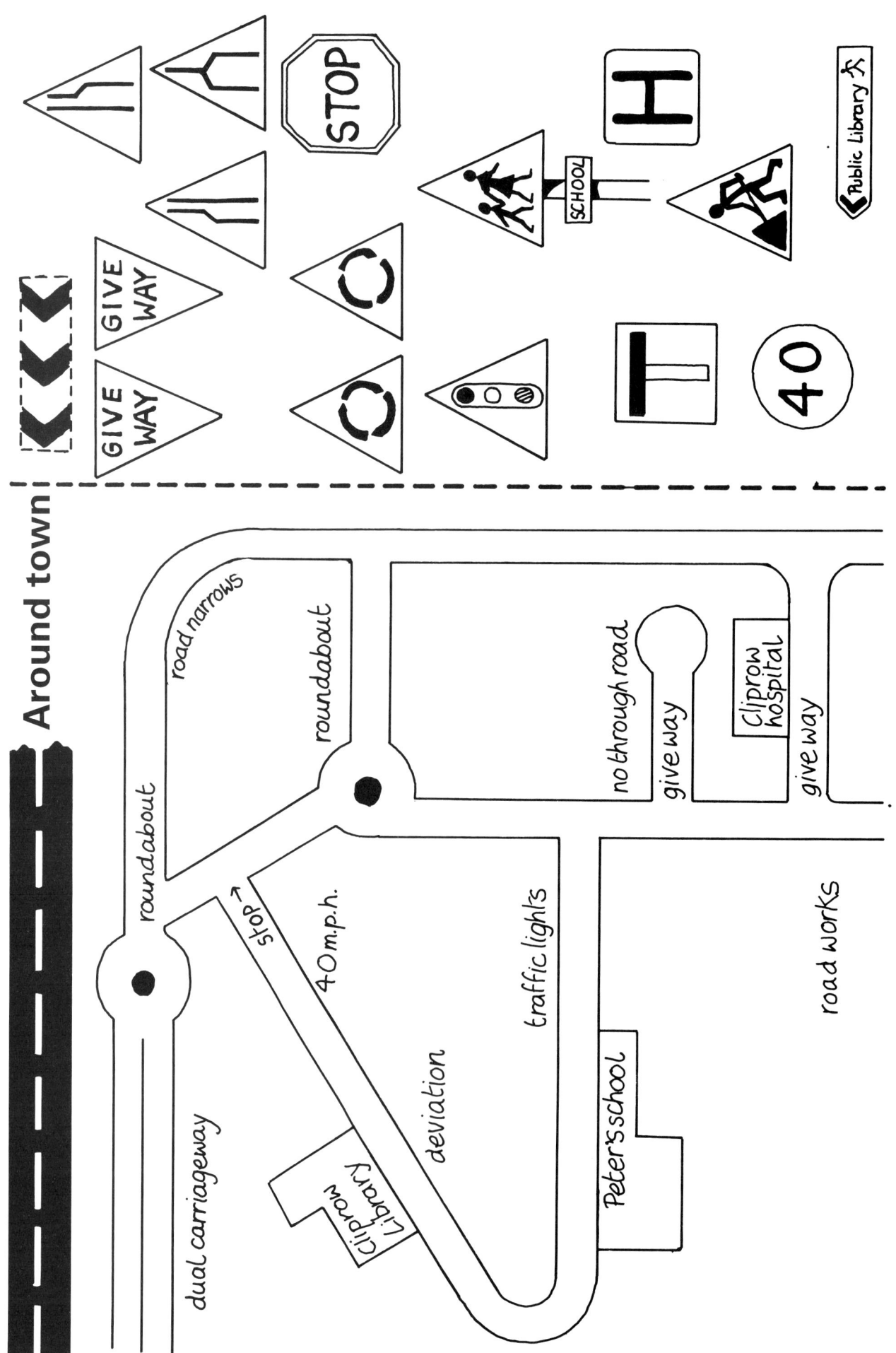

Around town

STOP

GIVE WAY

GIVE WAY

SCHOOL

Public Library

40

road narrows

roundabout

roundabout

no through road

give way

Cliprow hospital

give way

stop ↑

40 m.p.h.

traffic lights

road works

dual carriageway

Cliprow Library

deviation

Peter's school

54

Sign writing

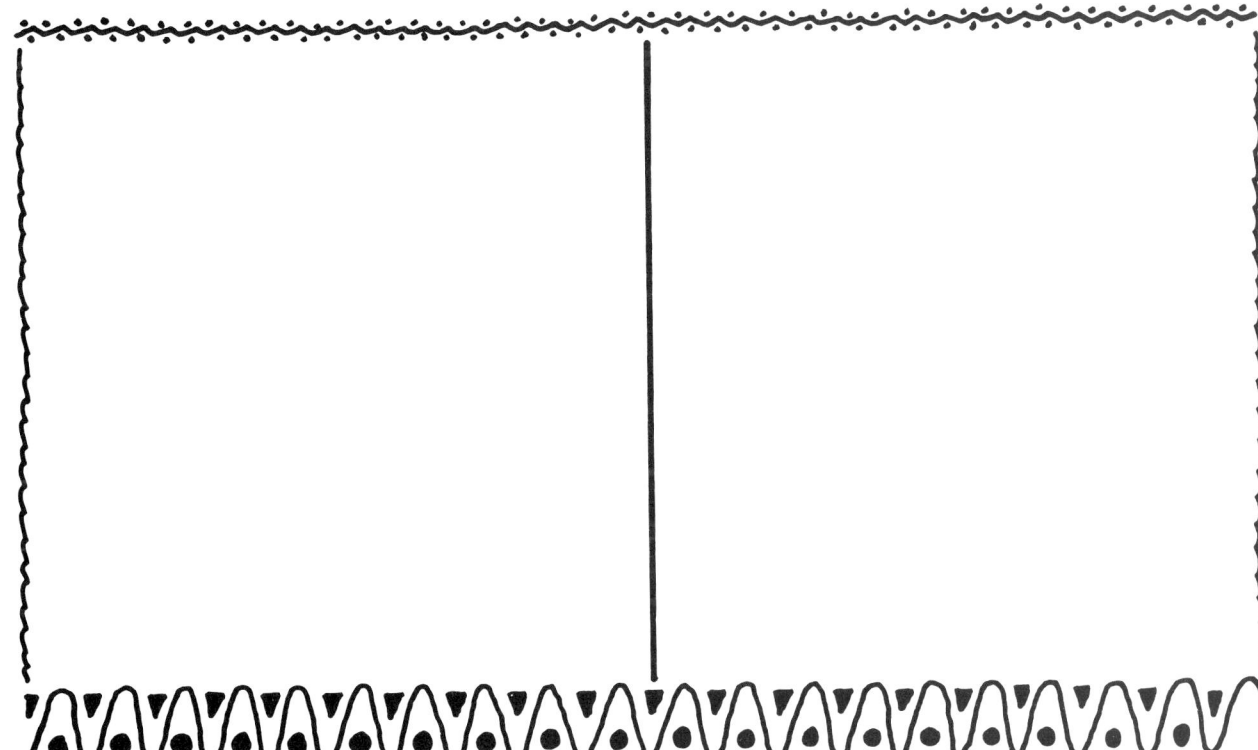

Egyptian	Meaning
	goose
	rolled parchment
	water
	mouth
	symbol of life
	quill

My signs	Meaning

Let's communicate C23

Tuning in

Programme type	Programme name	Time	Channel	Communication
Soap opera				
Sport				
Documentary				
Chat show				
Nature				
News				
Children's				

57

✓ Let's communicate C25

 # My rhythm piece

Title: _____

Mood: _____

Speed: _____

1.

2.

3.

4.

bang!   roll   shake   getting louder   getting softer

Let's communicate C24

Book/magazine assessment

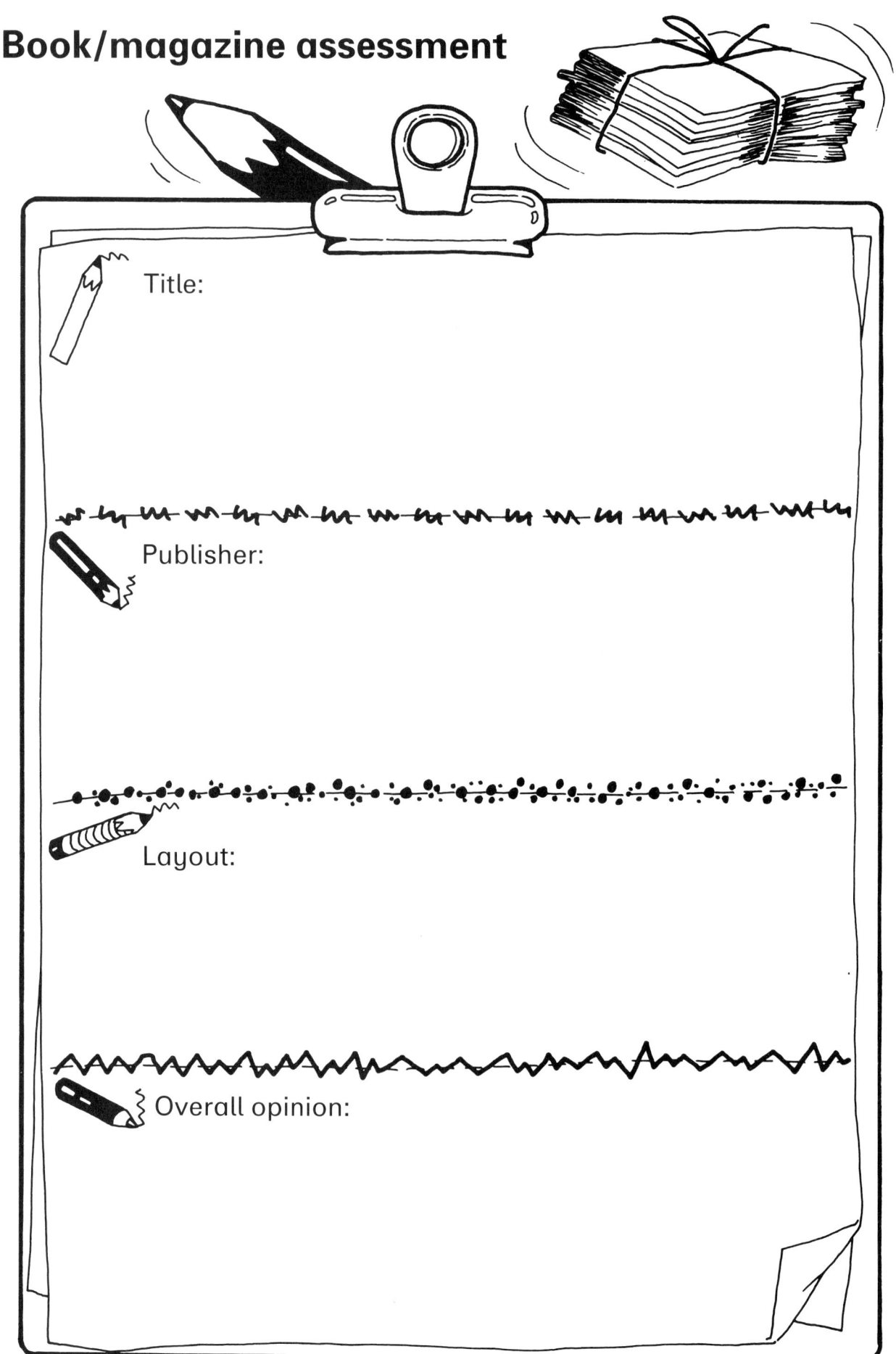

Title:

Publisher:

Layout:

Overall opinion:

Transport survey

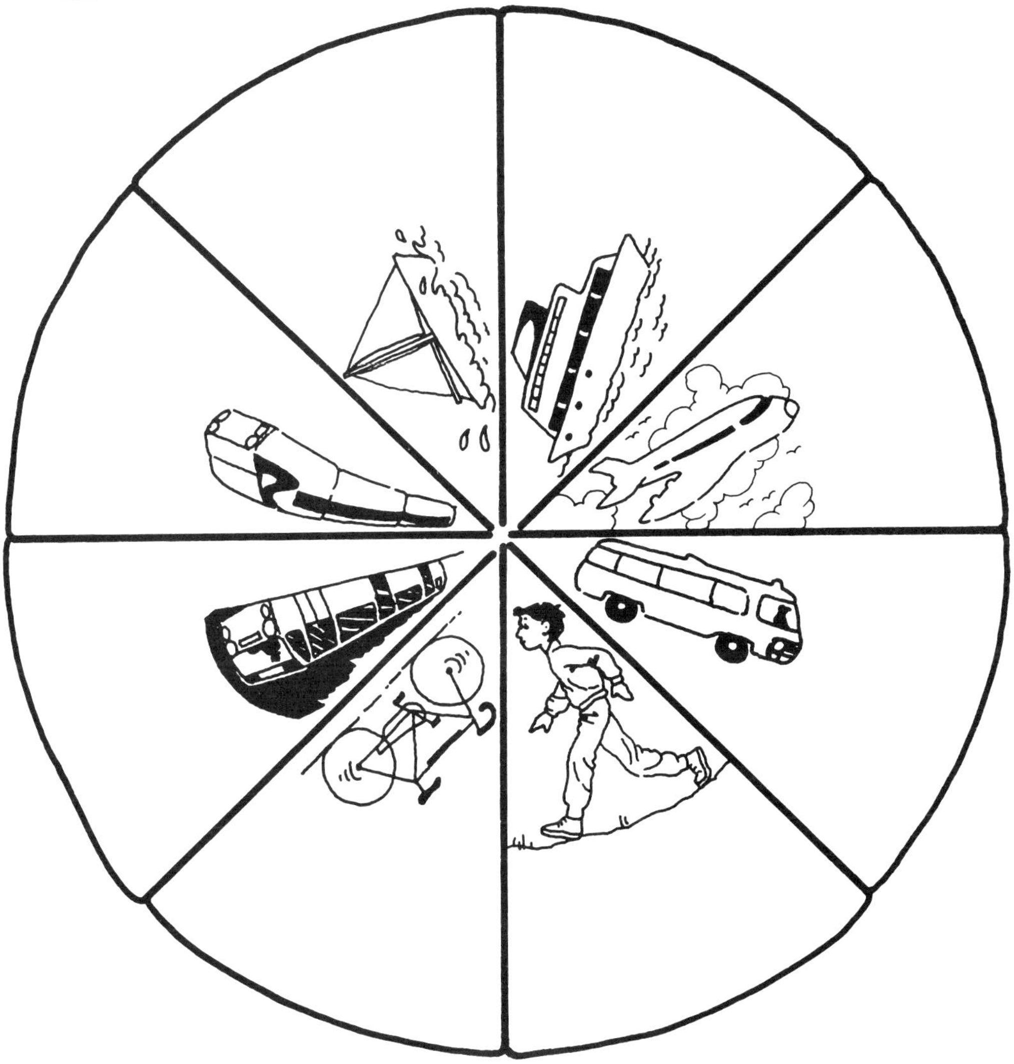

If you could choose one method of transport to travel locally,

what would it be? _____

Why? _____

_____

Which form of transport do you enjoy most? _____

_____

Why? _____

_____

Let's communicate C27

Faith symbols

name: _____

faith: _____

name: _____

faith: _____

name: _____

faith: _____

name: _____

faith: _____

name: _____

faith: _____

name: _____

faith: _____

Let's communicate C28

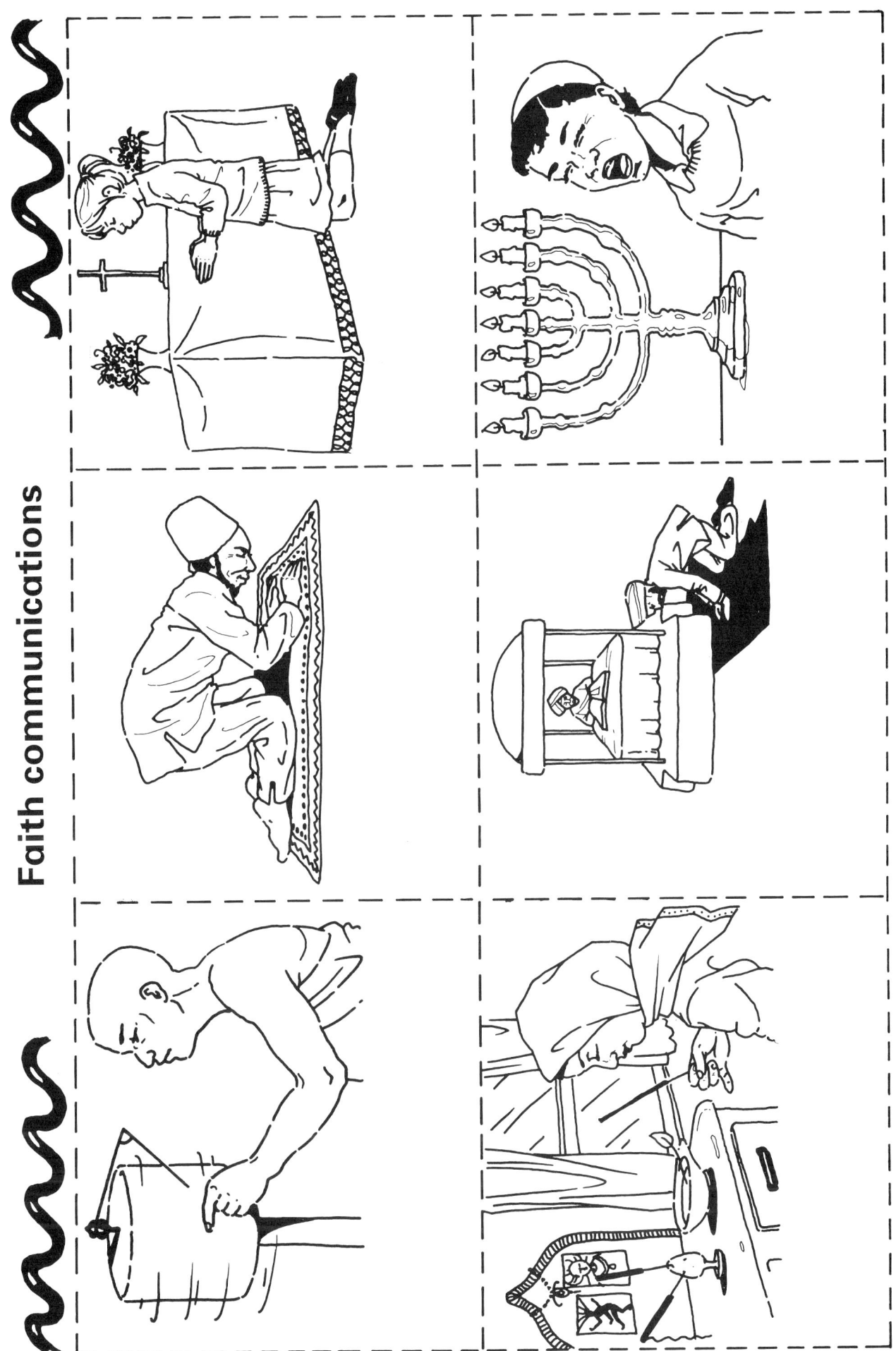

Faith communications

Let's communicate C29

My faith flower

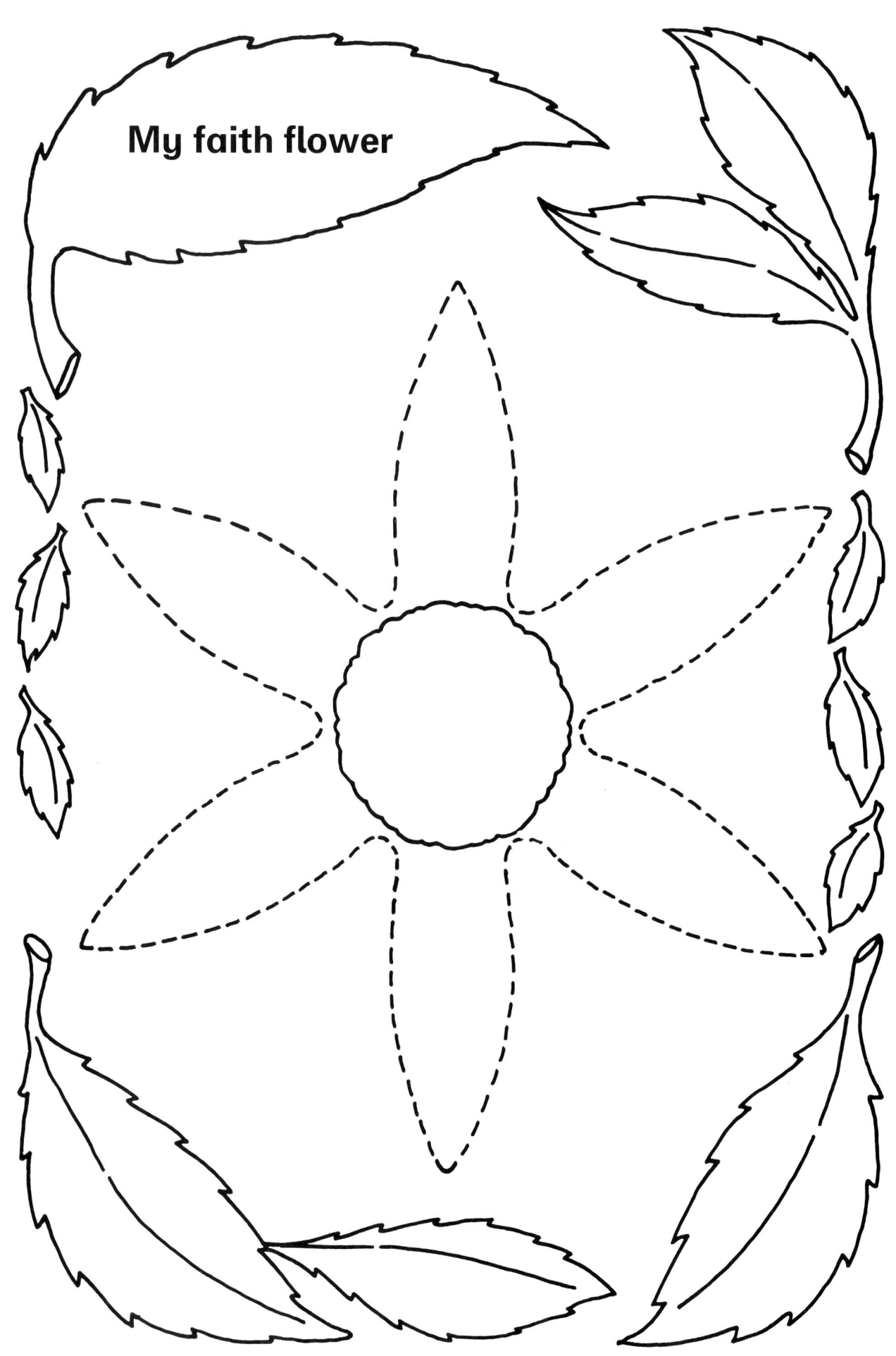

Let's communicate C30

Cross collection

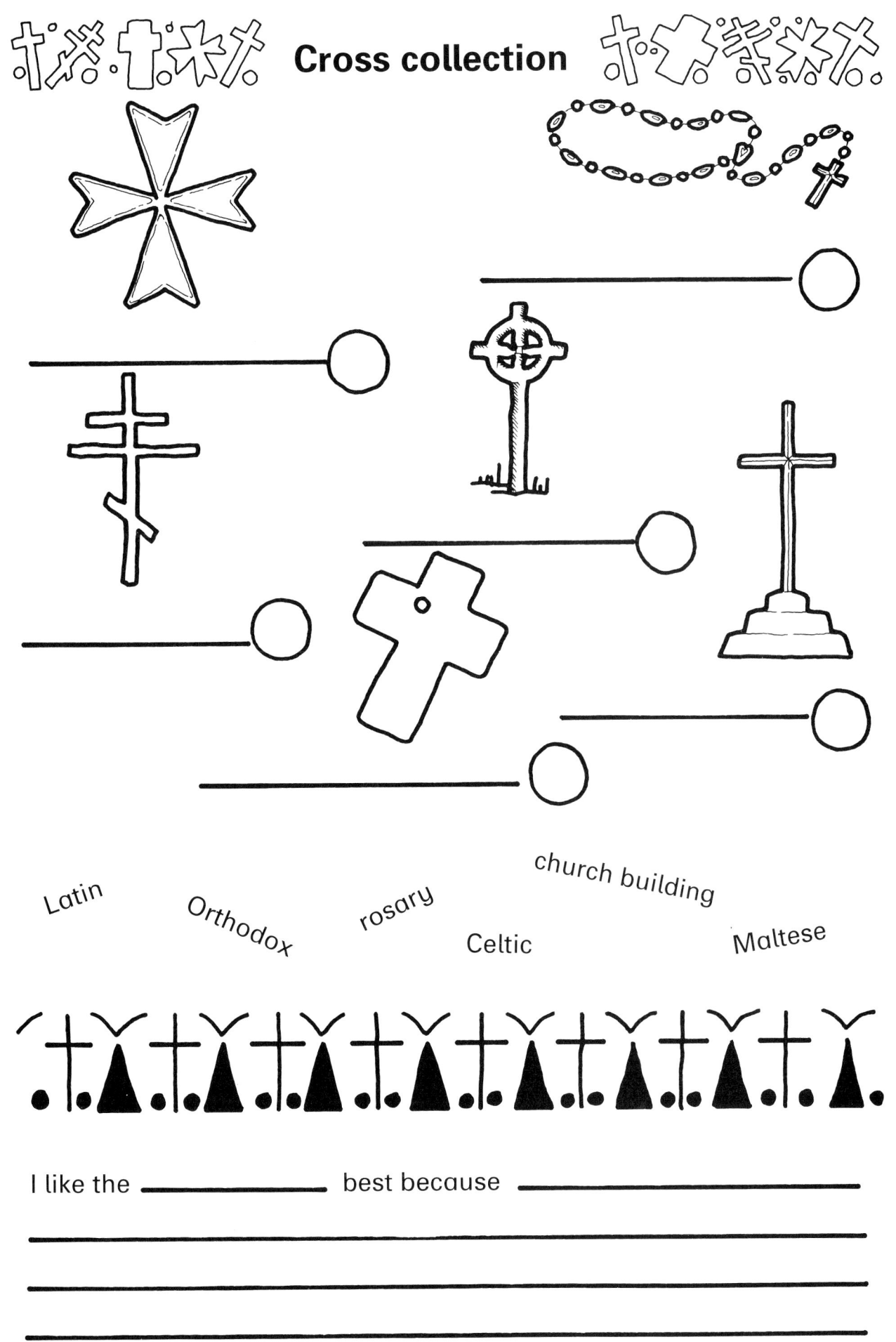

Latin

Orthodox

rosary

church building

Celtic

Maltese

I like the _____ best because _____

_____

_____

_____

✓ We believe C31

Bible bookcase 1

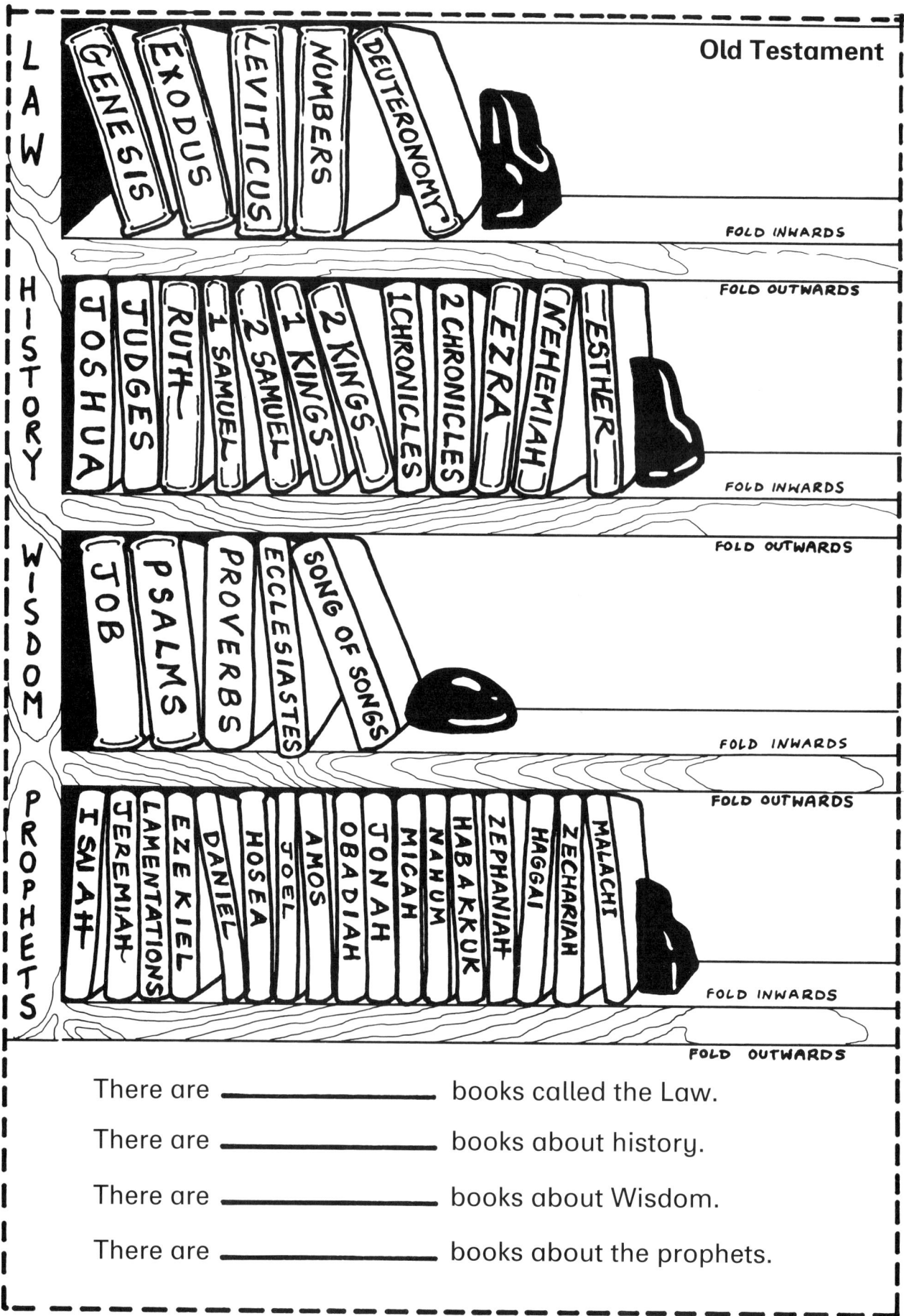

Old Testament

LAW

GENESIS
EXODUS
LEVITICUS
NUMBERS
DEUTERONOMY

FOLD INWARDS

FOLD OUTWARDS

HISTORY

JOSHUA
JUDGES
RUTH
1 SAMUEL
2 SAMUEL
1 KINGS
2 KINGS
1 CHRONICLES
2 CHRONICLES
EZRA
NEHEMIAH
ESTHER

FOLD INWARDS

FOLD OUTWARDS

WISDOM

JOB
PSALMS
PROVERBS
ECCLESIASTES
SONG OF SONGS

FOLD INWARDS

FOLD OUTWARDS

PROPHETS

ISAIAH
JEREMIAH
LAMENTATIONS
EZEKIEL
DANIEL
HOSEA
JOEL
AMOS
OBADIAH
JONAH
MICAH
NAHUM
HABAKKUK
ZEPHANIAH
HAGGAI
ZECHARIAH
MALACHI

FOLD INWARDS

FOLD OUTWARDS

There are _____ books called the Law.

There are _____ books about history.

There are _____ books about Wisdom.

There are _____ books about the prophets.

64

We believe C32

Bible bookcase 2

HISTORY

MATTHEW
MARK
LUKE
JOHN
ACTS

FOLD INWARDS

FOLD OUTWARDS

LETTERS

ROMANS
1 CORINTHIANS
2 CORINTHIANS
GALATIANS
EPHESIANS
PHILIPPIANS
COLOSSIANS
1 THESSALONIANS
2 THESSALONIANS
1 TIMOTHY
2 TIMOTHY
TITUS

FOLD INWARDS

FOLD OUTWARDS

LETTERS

PHILEMON
HEBREWS
JAMES
1 PETER
2 PETER
1 JOHN
2 JOHN
3 JOHN
JUDE
REVELATION

FOLD INWARDS

FOLD OUTWARDS

There are _____ books about history.

There are _____ books containing letters.

There are _____ books in the Old Testament.

There are _____ books in the New Testament.

There are _____ books altogether in the Bible

Christian artefacts

Christians drink wine from a chalice and eat bread, remembering Jesus' body and blood.

The candle is lit by Christians when they pray and worship.

The Bible is found in every church and is read by Christians.

The symbol of the cross reminds Christians of Jesus' death and how he brought new life.

Hymnbooks and prayer books are used by Christians in worship.

The bread, wine and candles are placed on the communion table.

We believe **C34**

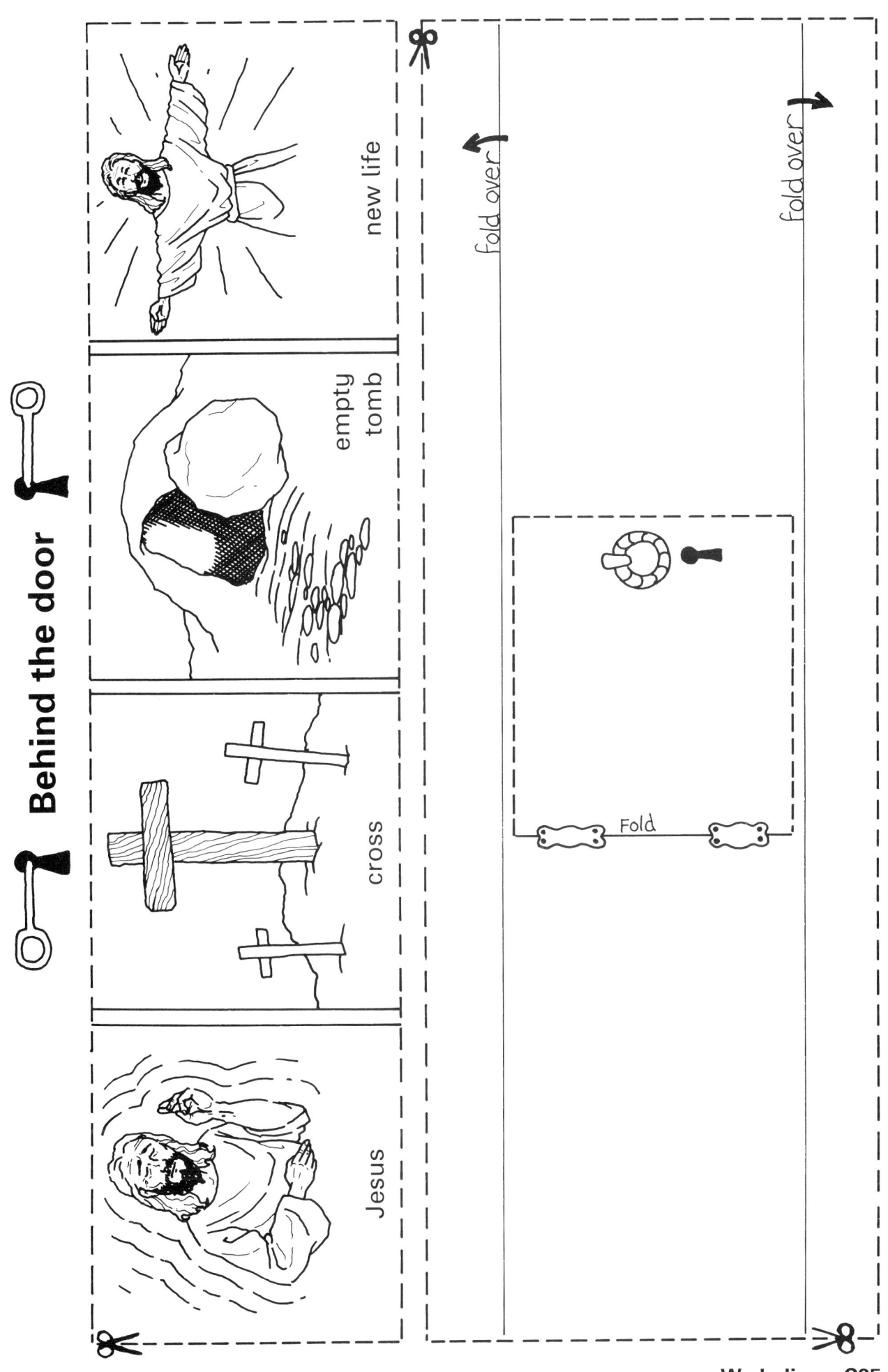

Behind the door

new life

empty tomb

cross

Jesus

fold over

fold over

Fold

Crescent and star

The Five Pillars

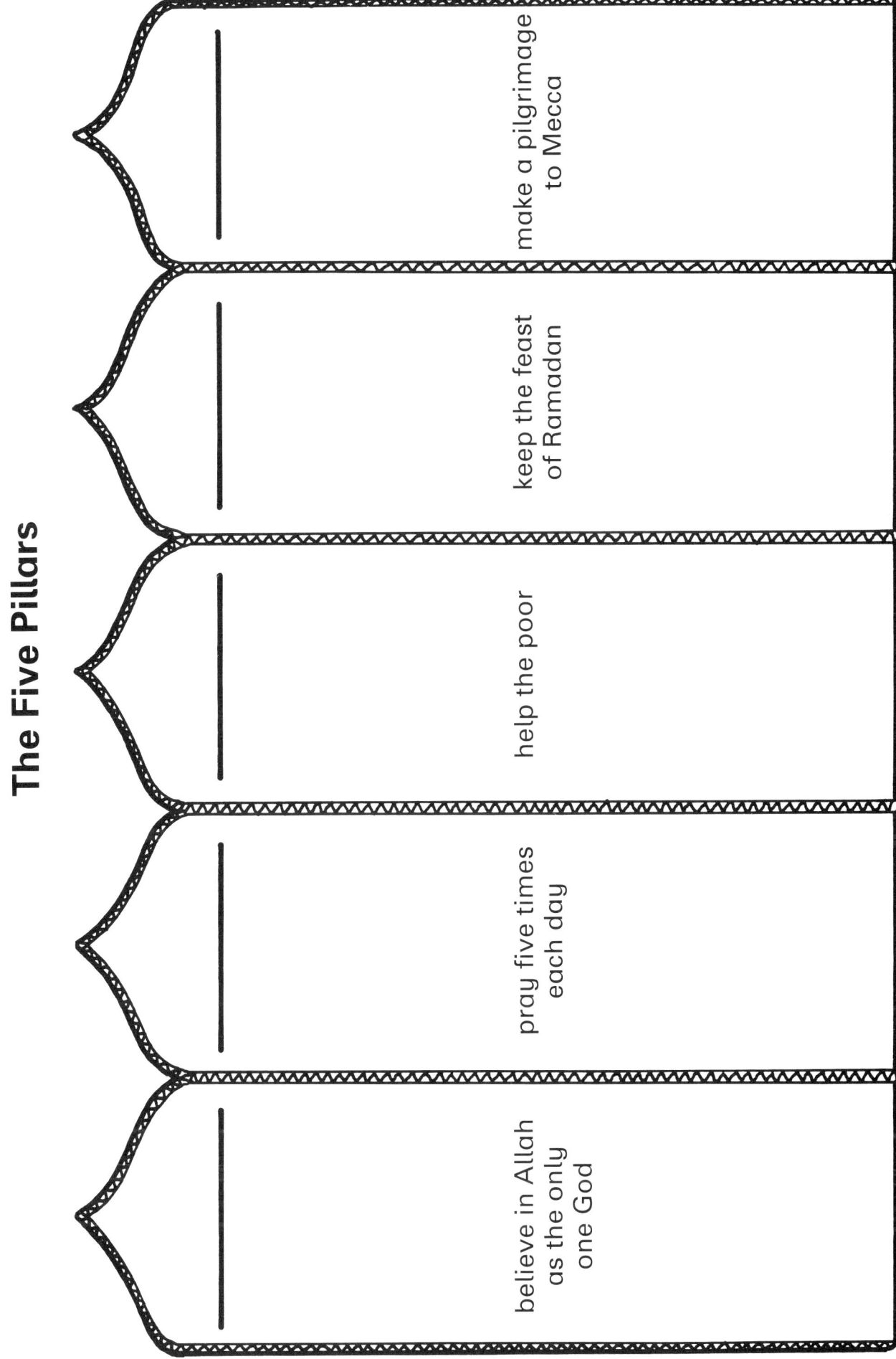

believe in Allah as the only one God

pray five times each day

help the poor

keep the feast of Ramadan

make a pilgrimage to Mecca

69

1. Love God.
2. Work hard.
3. Share your goods with the poor.

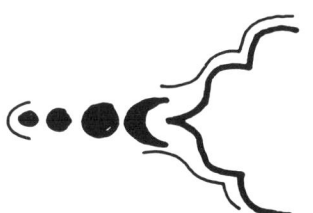

How could I work harder?

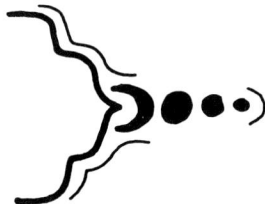

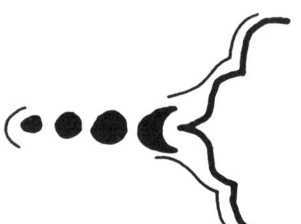

What could I give to the poor?

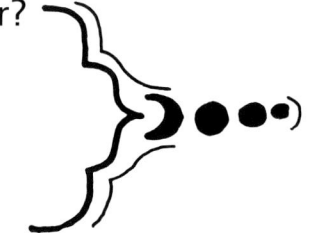

We believe C38

The Sikh gurus

1. Guru Nanak (1469–1539)
2. Guru Angad (1504–52)
3. Guru Amar Das (1479–1574)
4. Guru Ram Das (1534–81)
5. Guru Arjan (1563–1606)
6. Guru Har Gobind (1595–1644)
7. Guru Har Rai (1630–61)
8. Guru Har Krishen (1655–1664)
9. Guru Tegh Bahadur (1621–75)
10. Guru Gobind Singh (1666–1708)

We believe C39

Sikh vows

Aryan gods

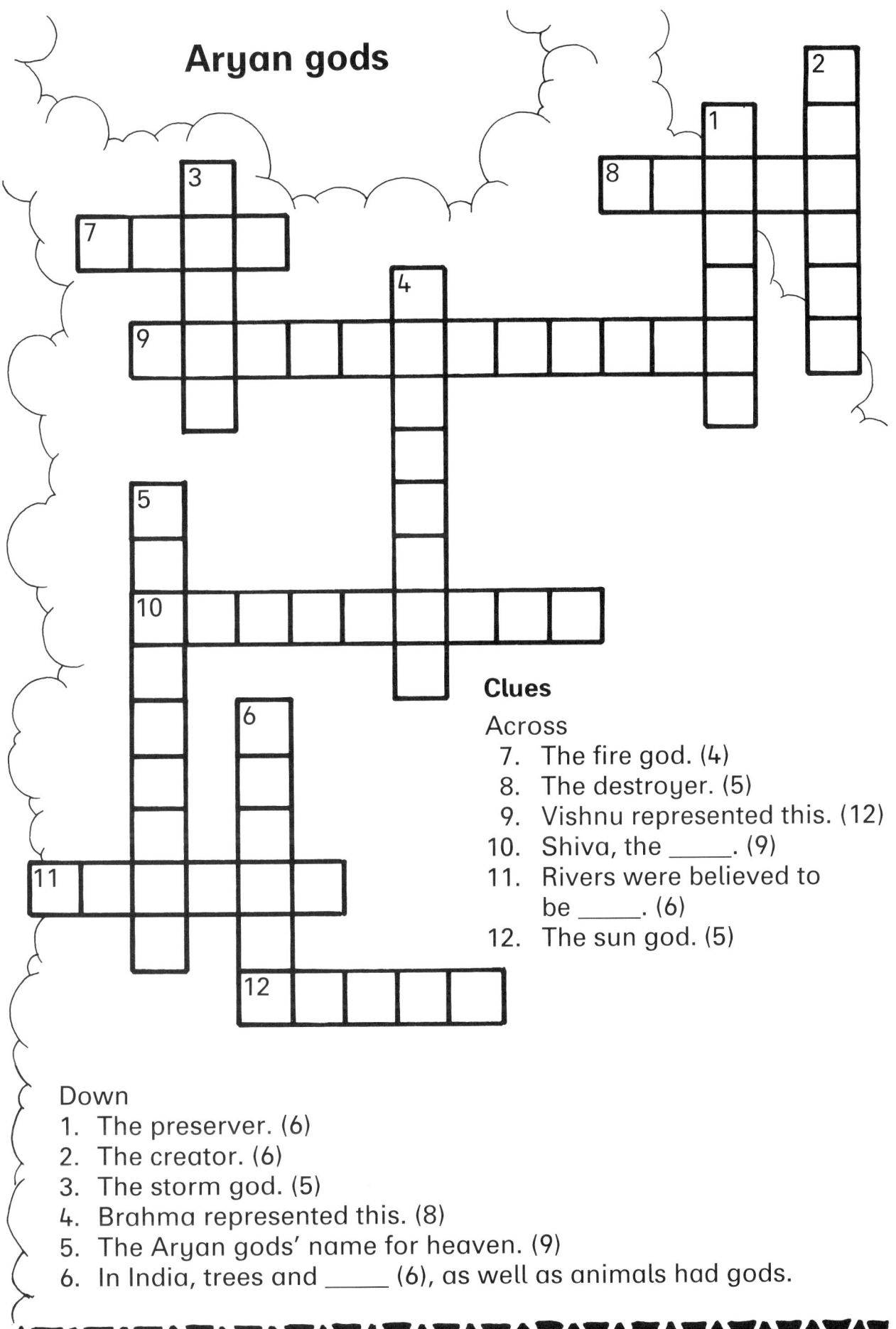

Clues

Across
7. The fire god. (4)
8. The destroyer. (5)
9. Vishnu represented this. (12)
10. Shiva, the _____. (9)
11. Rivers were believed to be _____. (6)
12. The sun god. (5)

Down
1. The preserver. (6)
2. The creator. (6)
3. The storm god. (5)
4. Brahma represented this. (8)
5. The Aryan gods' name for heaven. (9)
6. In India, trees and _____ (6), as well as animals had gods.

Different paths to God C41

 # Lakshmi

I am Lakshmi, the goddess of _____ and _____.

I bring these into every Hindu home every _____
festival time.

Light the way for me.

Different paths to God C42

Hindu home shrine

Different paths to God C43

Hindu trinity

Shiva

Vishnu

Brahma

Different paths to God C44

The caring prince

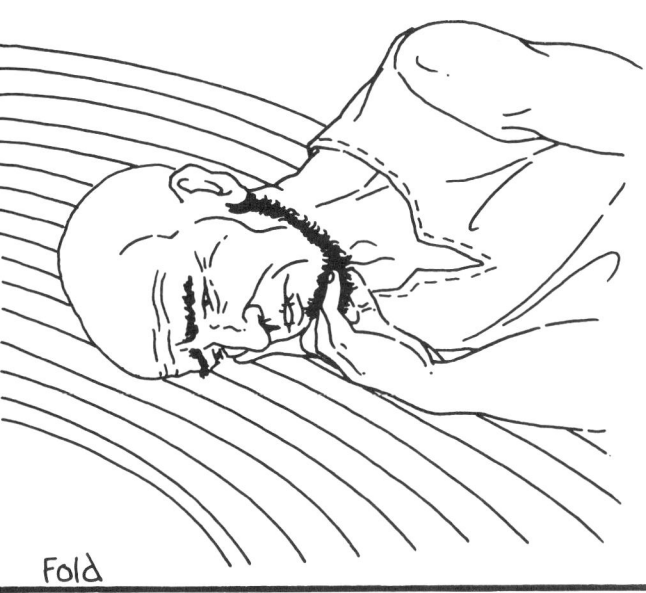

Fold

Siddartha's father worried about him. He wanted Siddartha to be a good king and not care too much. He decided that Siddartha, at the age of 16, should choose a wife.

One day, Siddartha's cousin injured a beautiful swan. He was unkind to animals. Siddartha looked after the swan until it was well again.

Fold

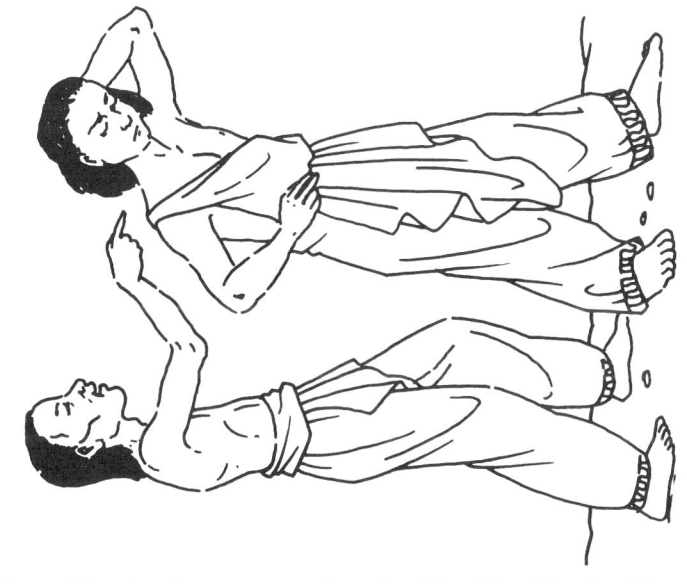

Prince Siddartha did not go hunting with his father and friends. His cousin was not kind and was always teasing him. He wanted to become king one day instead of Siddartha.

Different paths to God C45

Identify the Four Noble Sights.

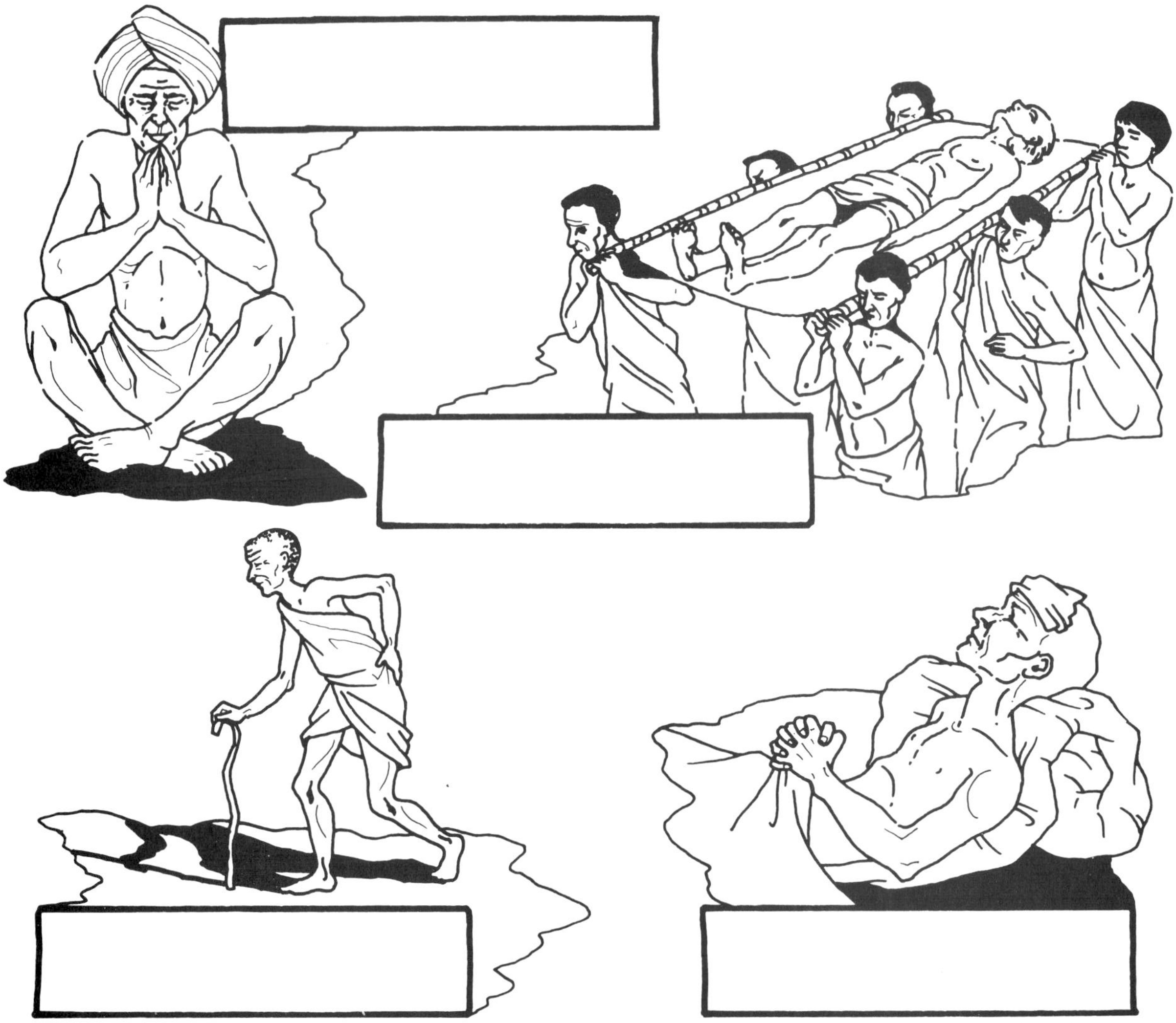

How I can help suffering in the world:

The Enlightenment story

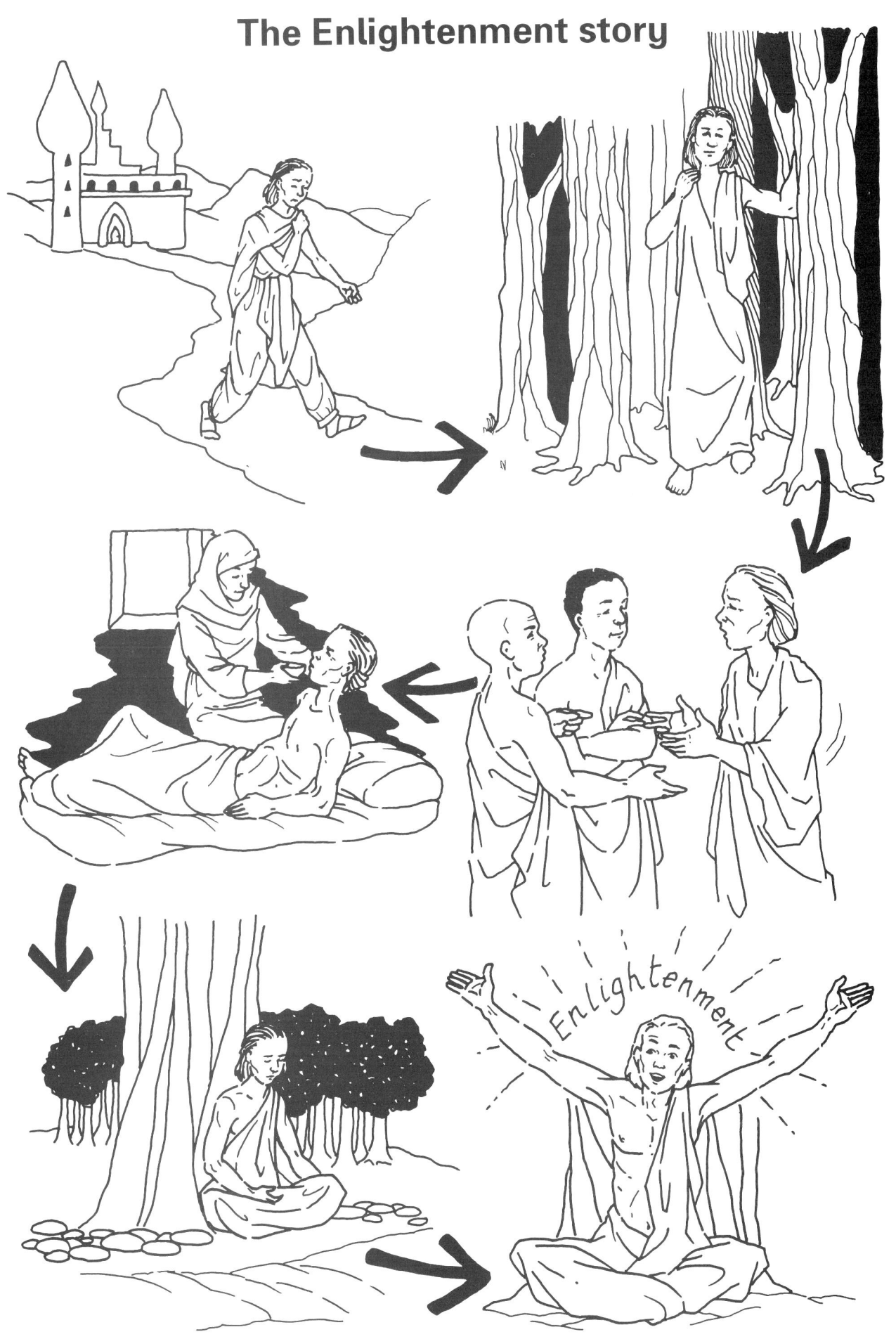

79

The Noble Eightfold Path

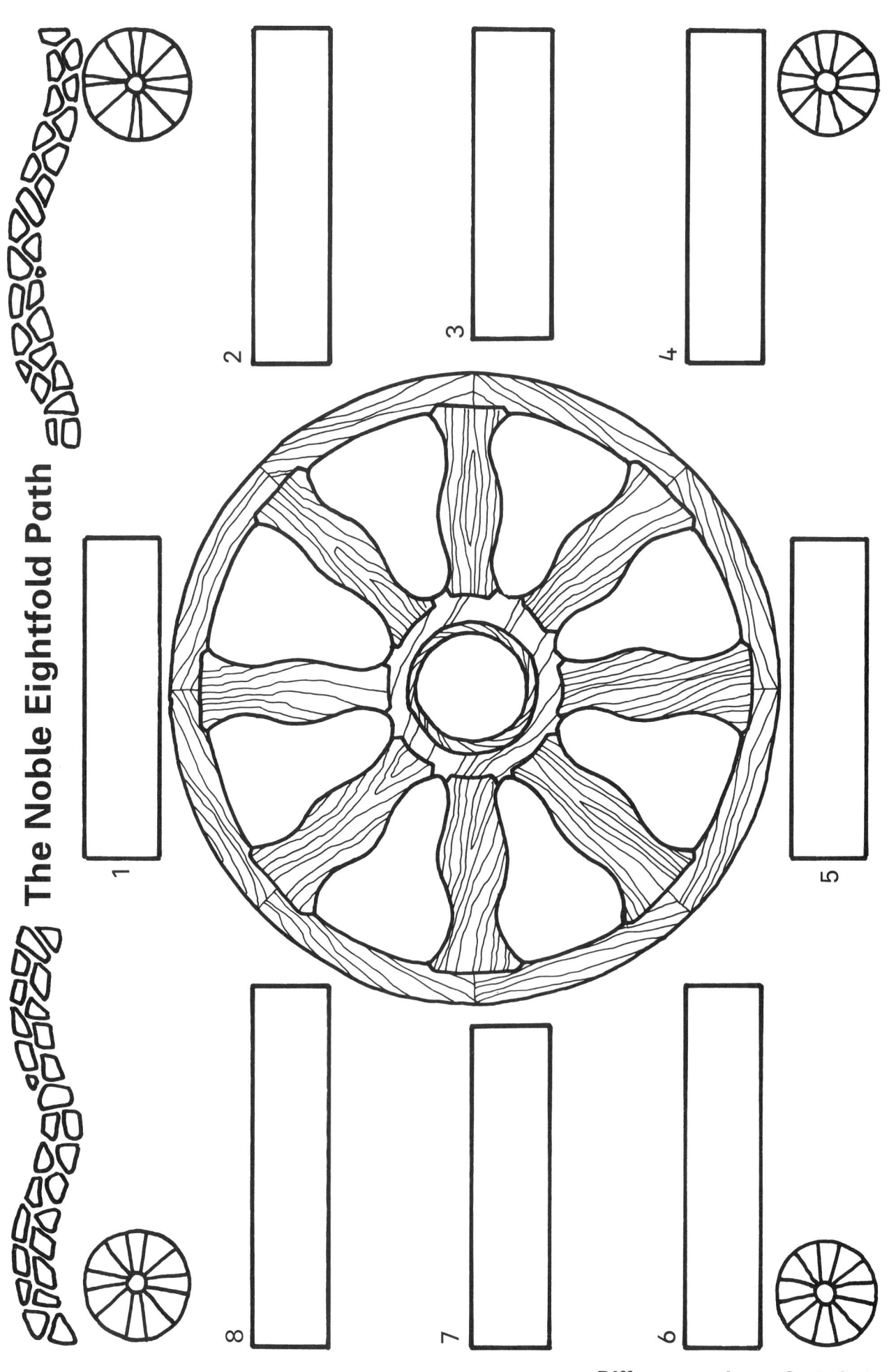

1

2

3

4

5

6

7

8

Different paths to God C48

Creating happiness

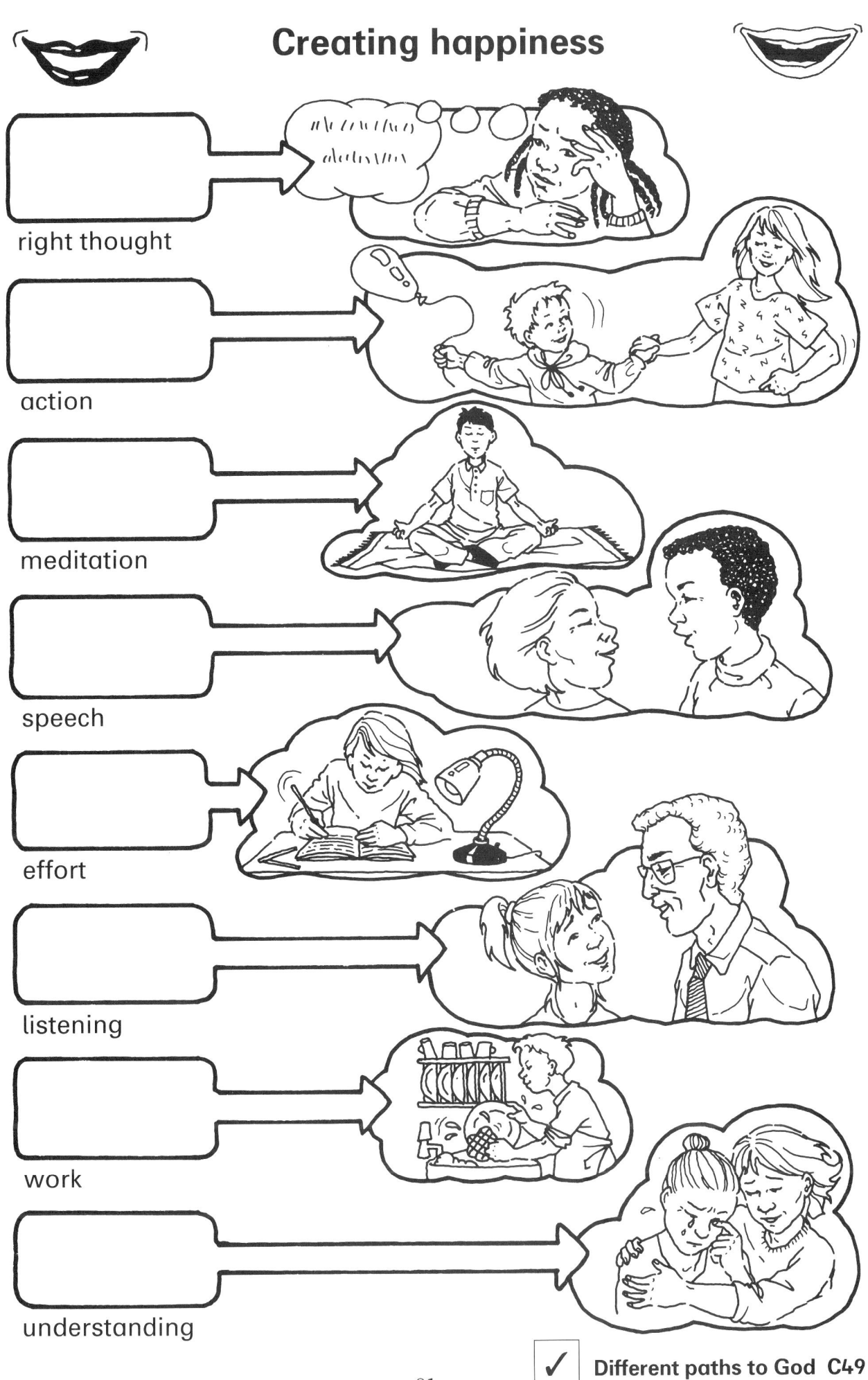

right thought

action

meditation

speech

effort

listening

work

understanding

81

The Buddhist way

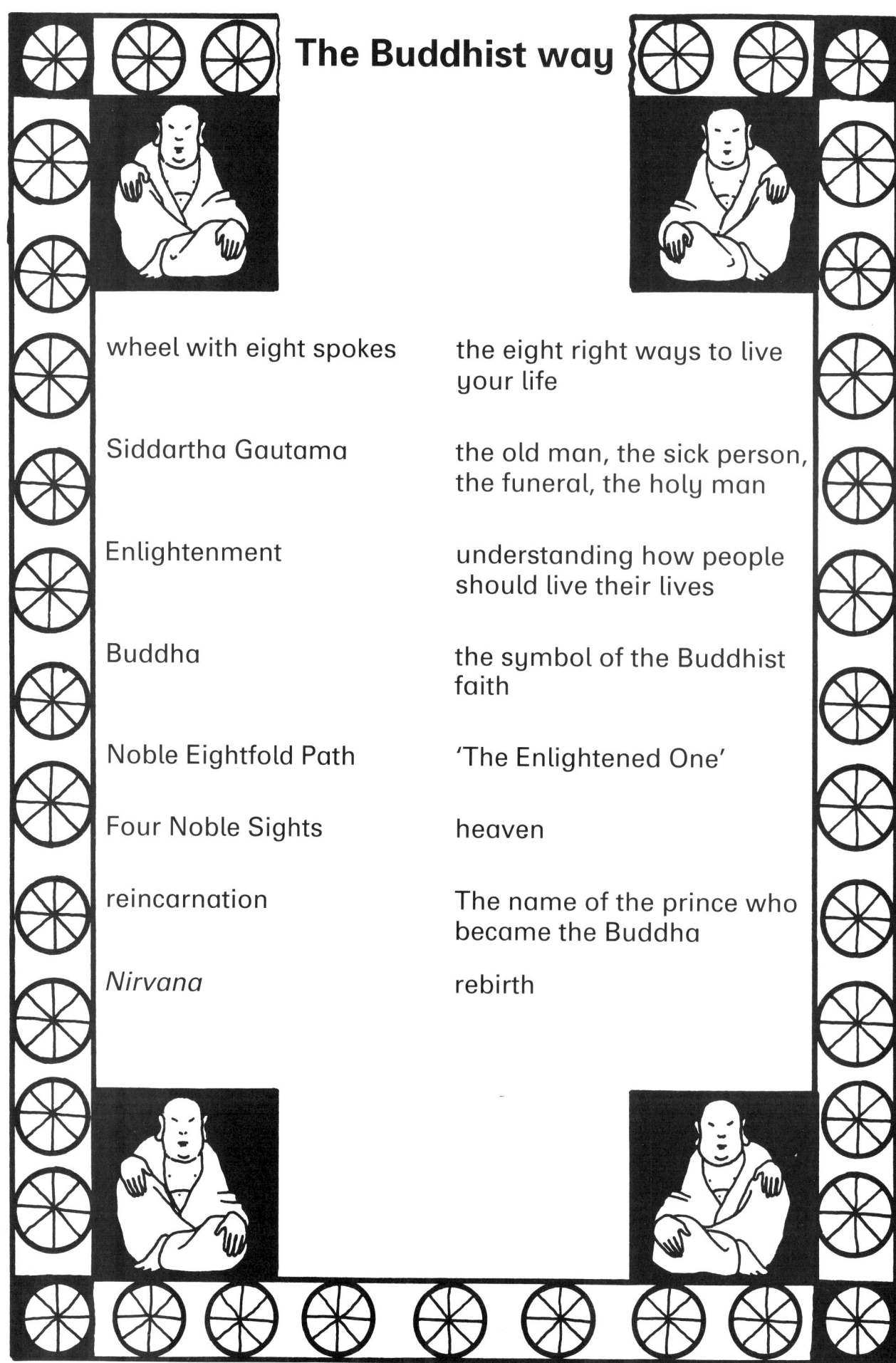

wheel with eight spokes	the eight right ways to live your life
Siddartha Gautama	the old man, the sick person, the funeral, the holy man
Enlightenment	understanding how people should live their lives
Buddha	the symbol of the Buddhist faith
Noble Eightfold Path	'The Enlightened One'
Four Noble Sights	heaven
reincarnation	The name of the prince who became the Buddha
Nirvana	rebirth

Different paths to God   C50

Khadijah's devotion

Khadijah gave a man called _____ the job of her _____.

Khadijah was a _____ and was very _____.

Traders travelled through the desert, with _____ and _____ produced in Khadijah's _____.

She married him. He became a _____ of Islam. She was a _____ and _____ wife.

Sacred lives C51

Friendship

Akbar showed friendship.

He was a humble man.

He was a man of peace.

He spoke to everybody, whatever their position in life.

He looked after his people and made sure they were safe.

What about me?

Am I like Emperor Akbar?

Am I modest, not proud?

Do I search for peace?

Do I ever argue and fight?

Do I speak to everyone I know as their friend?

How can I show true friendship to others?

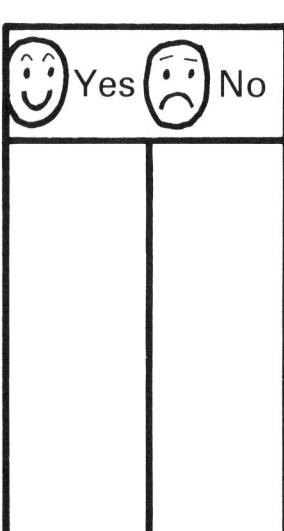

🙂 Yes	🙁 No

The Golden Temple

Sacred lives C53

My life line

5   10   15   20   25   30   35   40   45   50   55   60   65   Over 65

Sacred lives C54

Vir Singh was born in Amritsar in the year 1872.

He was the most famous ——————

and poet in the Punjab region of India.

He set up a printing press for the Khalsa

brotherhood of Sikhs, which published ——————.

In 1899, he began a Sikh ——————.

He cared about his community and set up a

widows' home, a home for the ——————

and a Khalsa ——————.

Vir Singh called God '——————!'

Wonderful Lord!

Gandhi scroll

GANDHI

All people should do their duty to others

All people are equal

All people should lead simple lives without harming others

How can we help?

What we could do

Description

Sacred lives C57

Four caring Christians

Sally Trench

Eric Liddell

Robert Kemble

Jean Vanier

Stop and go

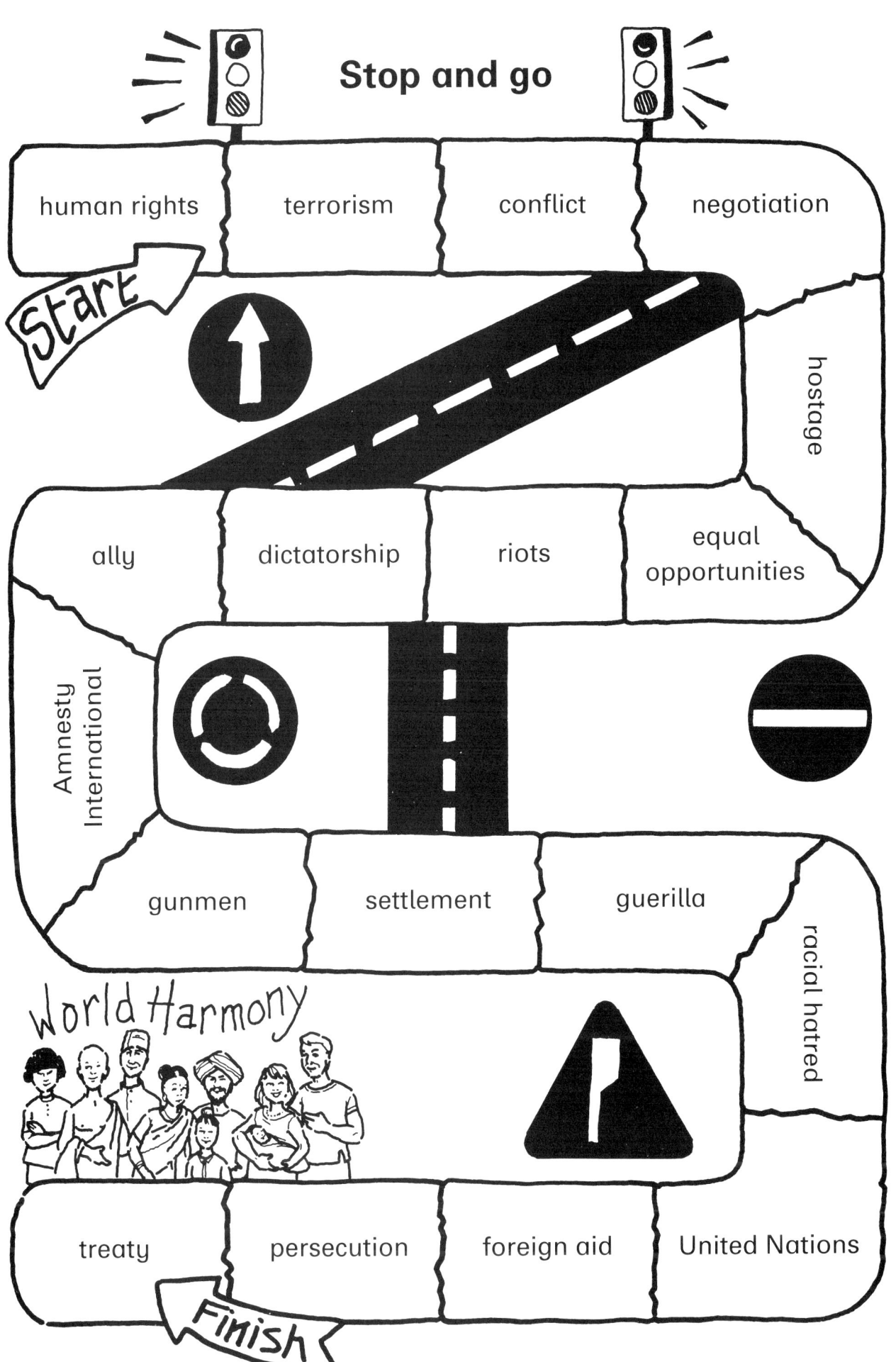

Start

human rights · terrorism · conflict · negotiation

hostage

ally · dictatorship · riots · equal opportunities

Amnesty International

gunmen · settlement · guerilla

racial hatred

World Harmony

treaty · persecution · foreign aid · United Nations

Finish

Doing good to others trail

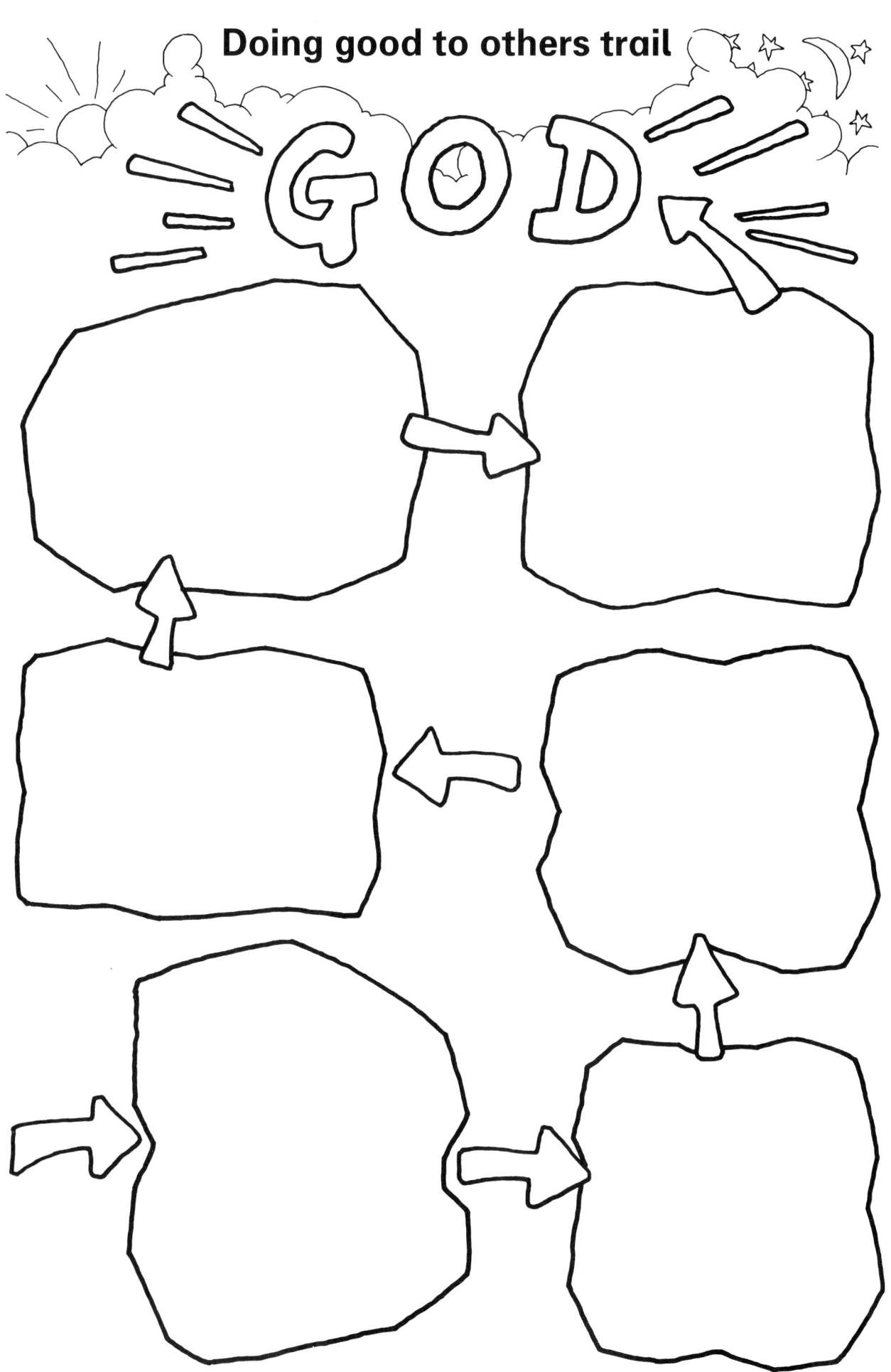

The three arrivals 1

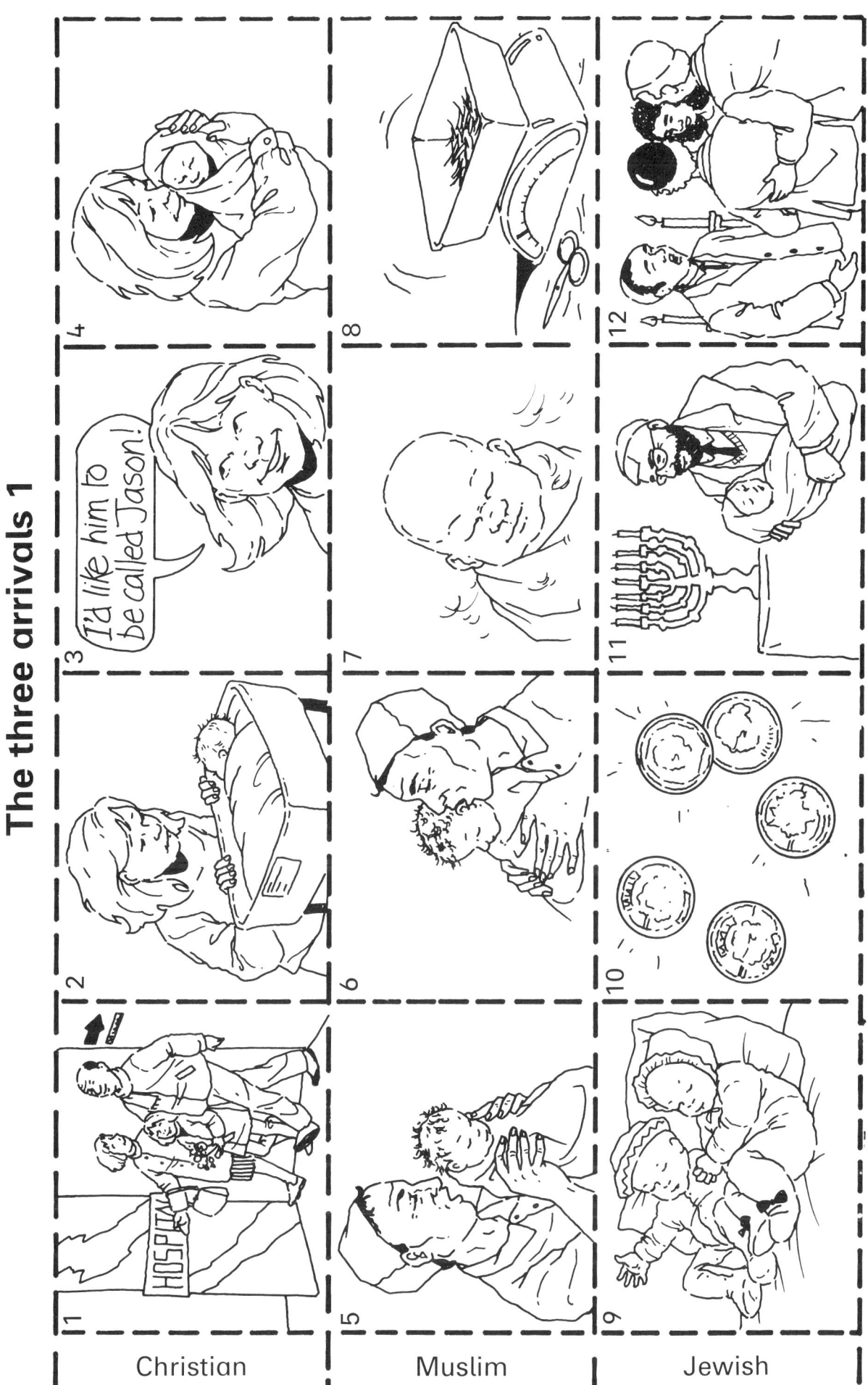

1 Anna went with Gran and Grandad to the hospital.

2 She saw her baby brother asleep in a cradle by her mother's bed.

3 She wanted him to be called Jason.

4 She could now love and care for Jason as his big sister.

5 Soon after he was born, baby Asif's father spoke the *adhan* or call to prayer into his right ear.

6 A prayer about the greatness of God was spoken into his left ear.

7 After a family party and readings, baby Asif's head was shaved.

8 His hair was weighed and an amount of money equal to this was given to charity.

9 The family felt happy and blessed when the Jewish twins, Jacob and Ruth, were born.

10 After circumcision at eight days, Jacob was offered to a Jewish family and 'bought back' for five silver coins.

11 Ruth's name was officially given to her at the synagogue on the Sabbath following her birth.

12 All the family gave thanks to God for the twins. They sang songs and said prayers.

Endings C62

I need ...

Thank you

Flame

Infants to Juniors

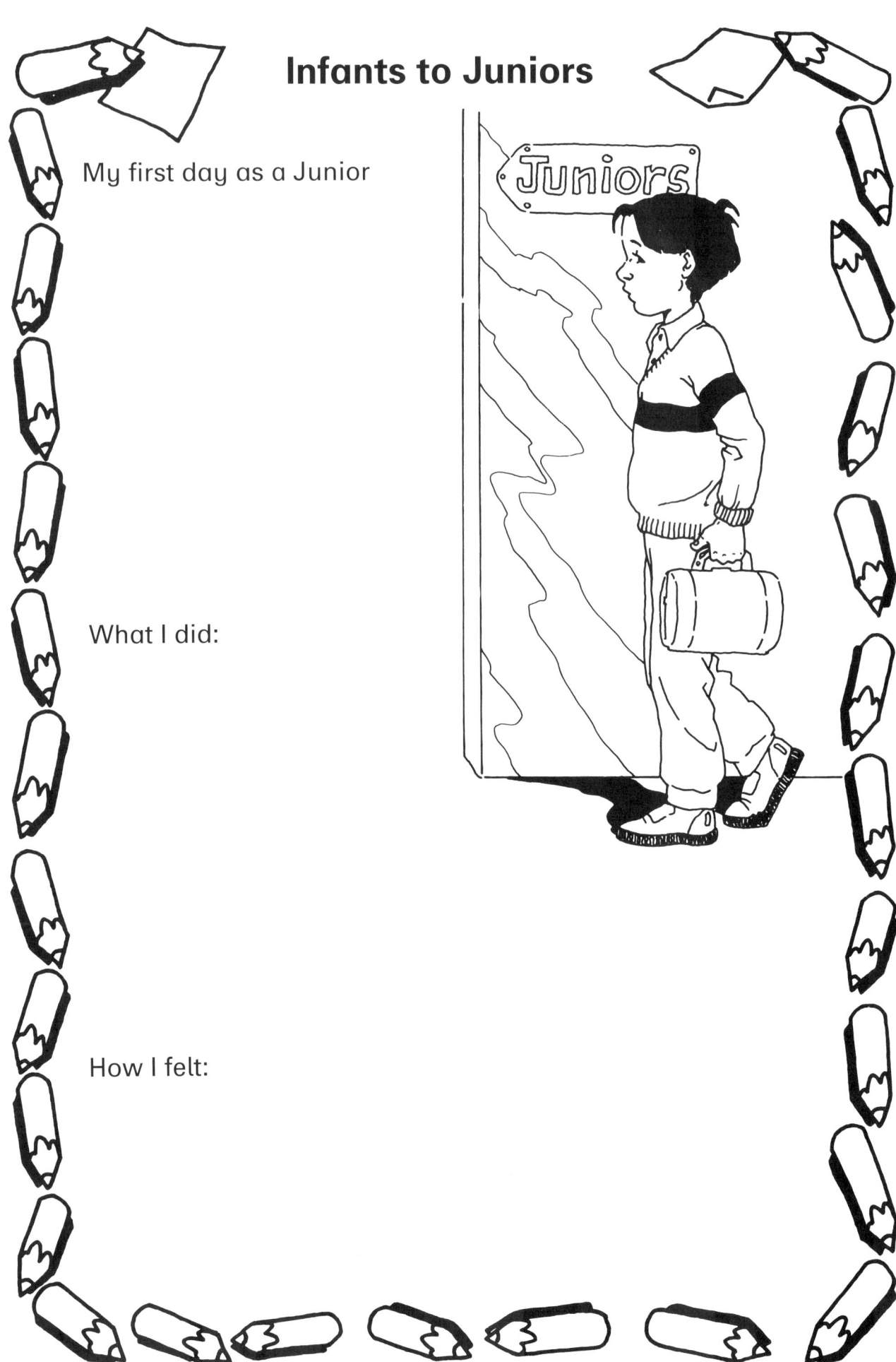

My first day as a Junior

What I did:

How I felt:

Endings C64

Endings cube

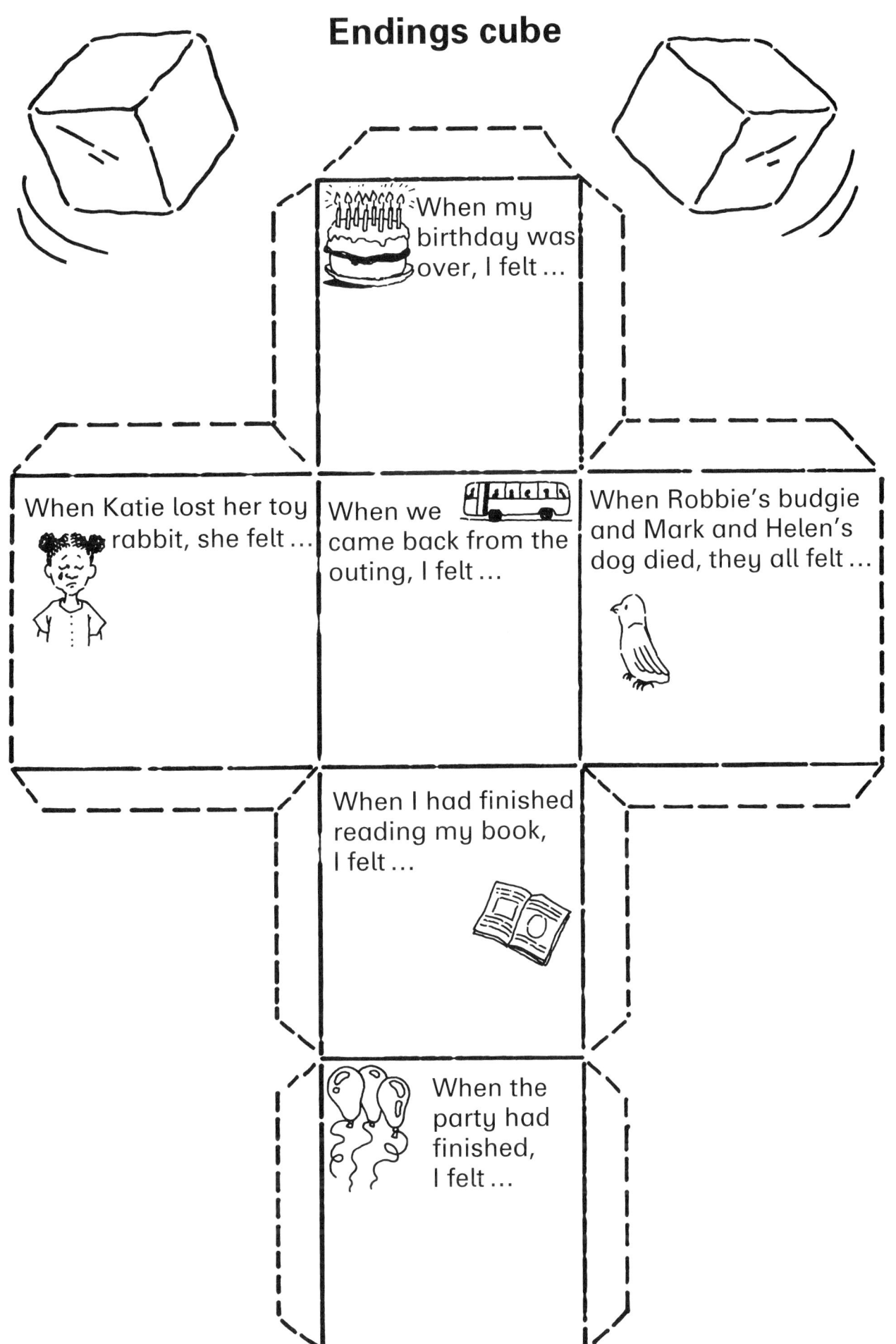

When my birthday was over, I felt ...

When Katie lost her toy rabbit, she felt ...

When we came back from the outing, I felt ...

When Robbie's budgie and Mark and Helen's dog died, they all felt ...

When I had finished reading my book, I felt ...

When the party had finished, I felt ...

Endings C65

In loving memory

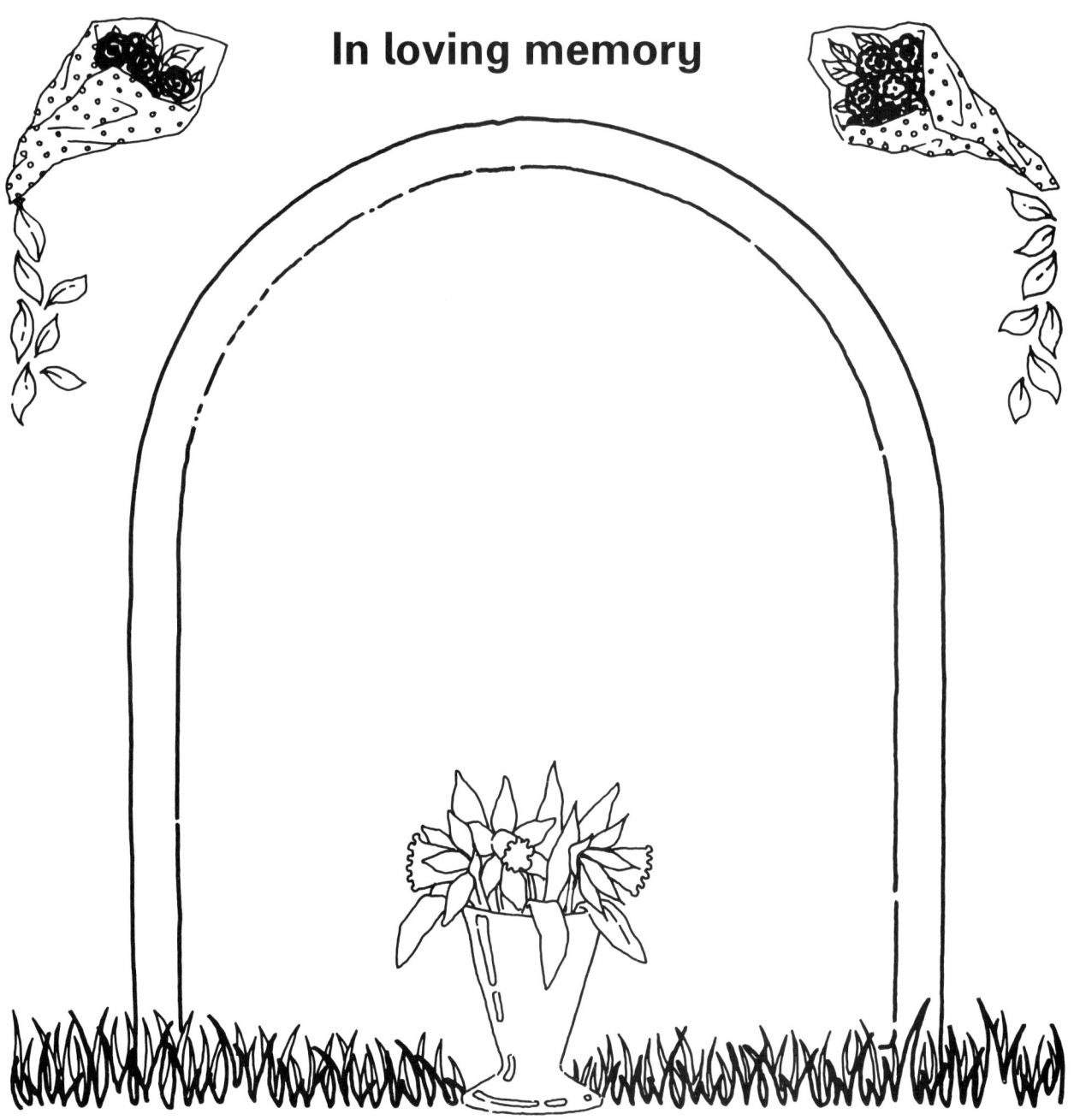

This person's appearance and character:

This person's family:

Endings C66

Death beliefs

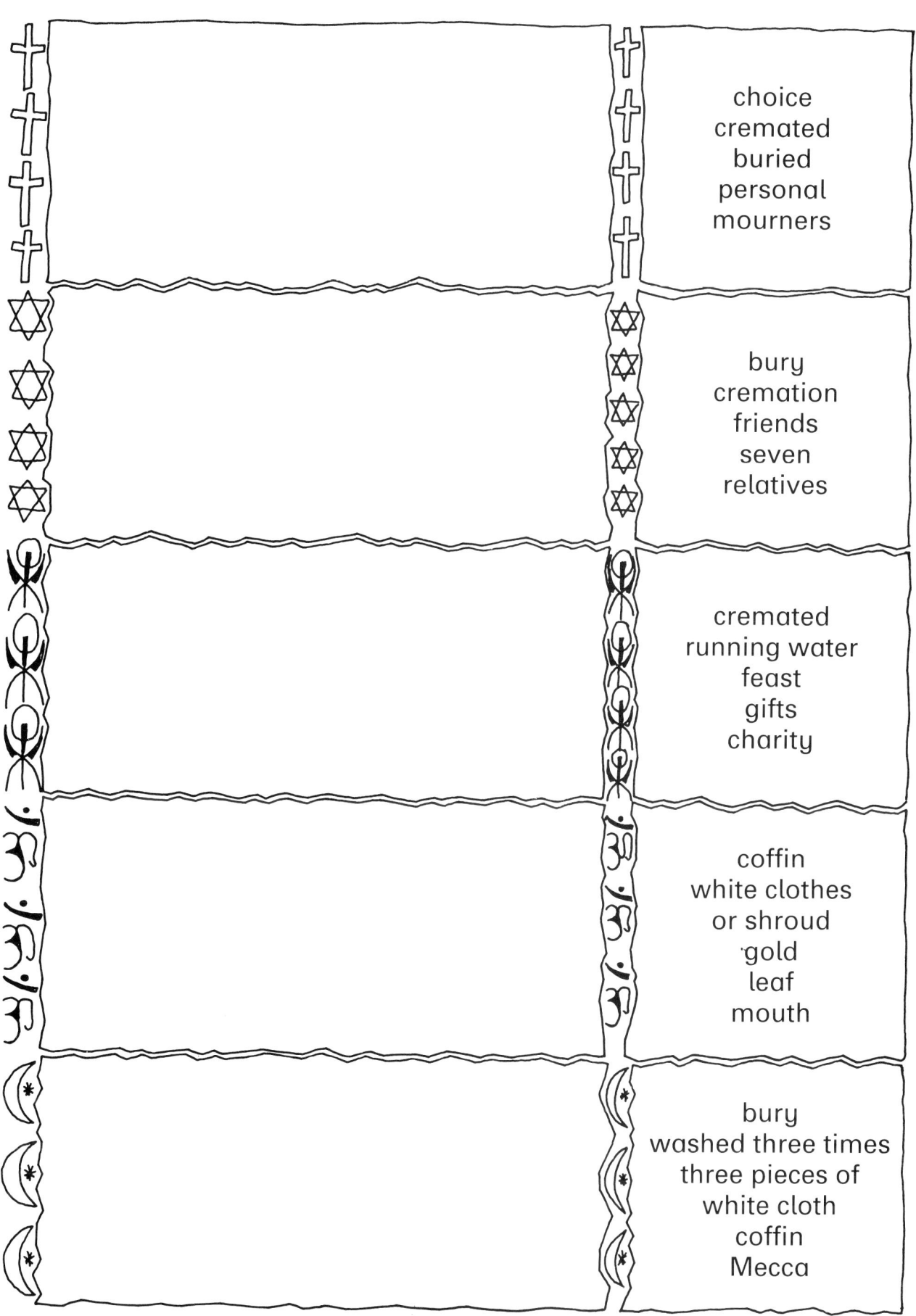

	choice cremated buried personal mourners
	bury cremation friends seven relatives
	cremated running water feast gifts charity
	coffin white clothes or shroud gold leaf mouth
	bury washed three times three pieces of white cloth coffin Mecca

Afterlife beliefs

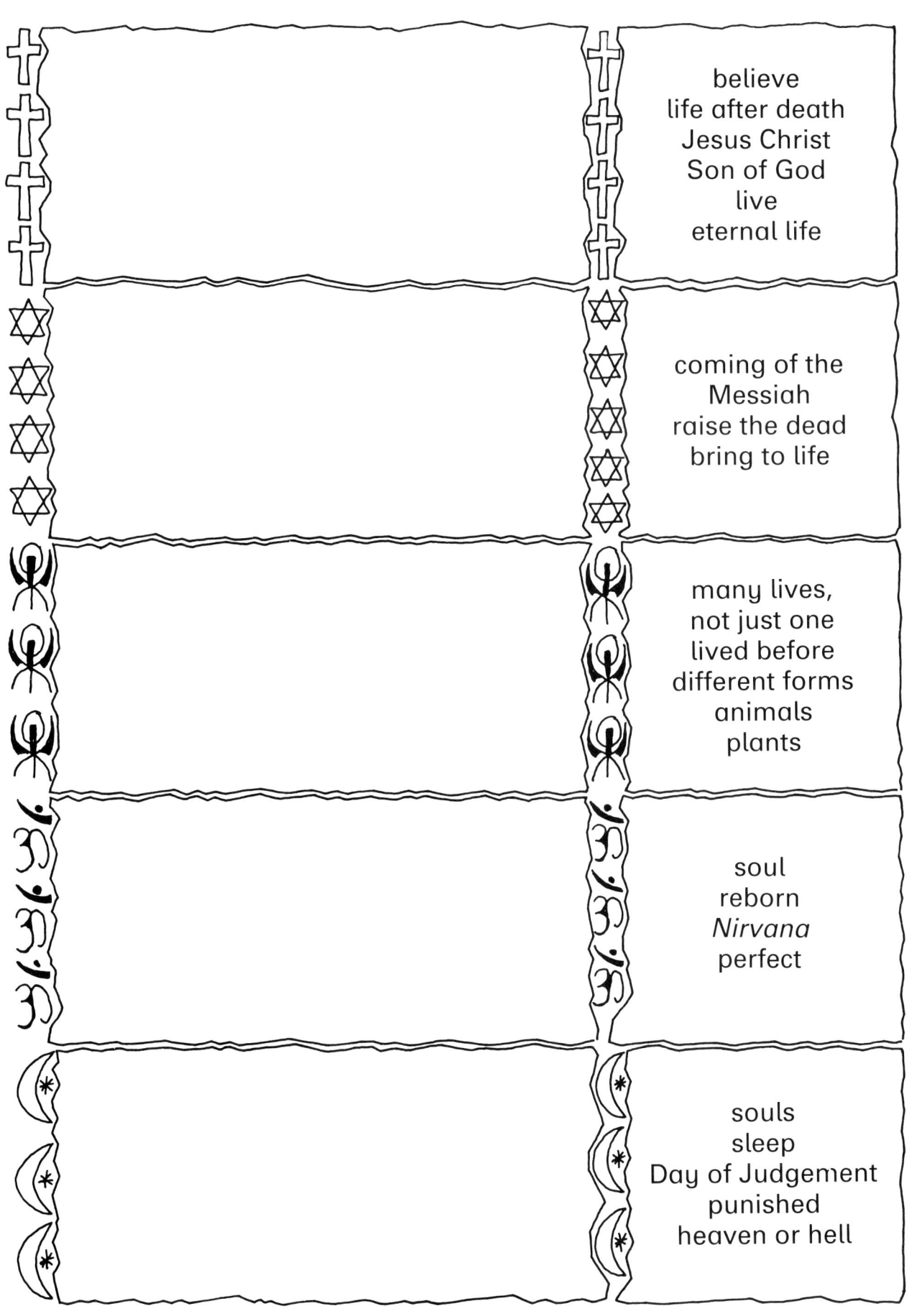

believe
life after death
Jesus Christ
Son of God
live
eternal life

coming of the
Messiah
raise the dead
bring to life

many lives,
not just one
lived before
different forms
animals
plants

soul
reborn
Nirvana
perfect

souls
sleep
Day of Judgement
punished
heaven or hell

Endings C68

My sympathy card

Expressing grief

Who will heal me?

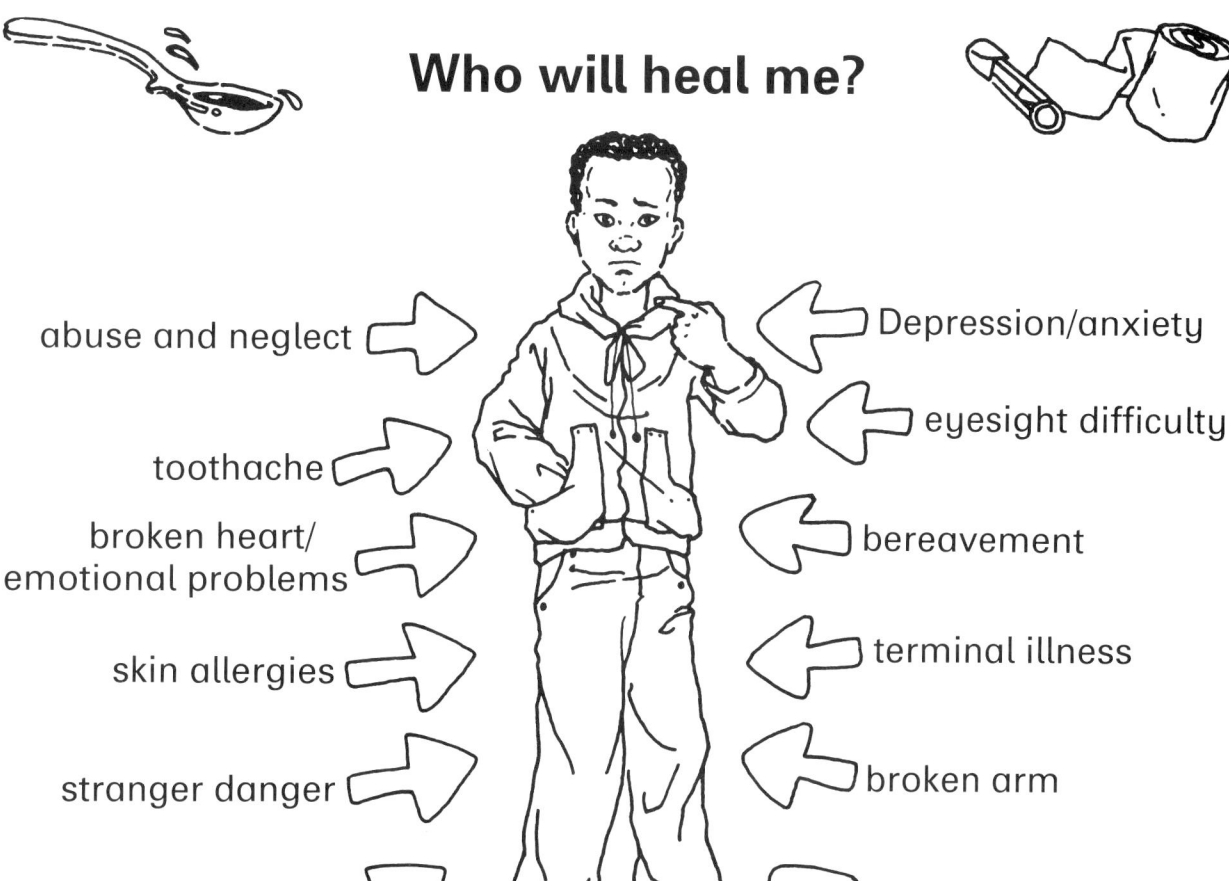

abuse and neglect

Depression/anxiety

eyesight difficulty

toothache

broken heart/
emotional problems

bereavement

skin allergies

terminal illness

stranger danger

broken arm

'flu

slight upset

Agency	Item(s)	Agency	Item(s)
dentist		ambulance	
family doctor		family/parents	
police		Childline	
religious guide		faith healer	
hospital		counsellor	
optician		homeopath	

✓ **Healing C71**

Hospital visit

Find out which part of the body each of these departments specialises in treating. Make a list on paper.

Caring for teeth

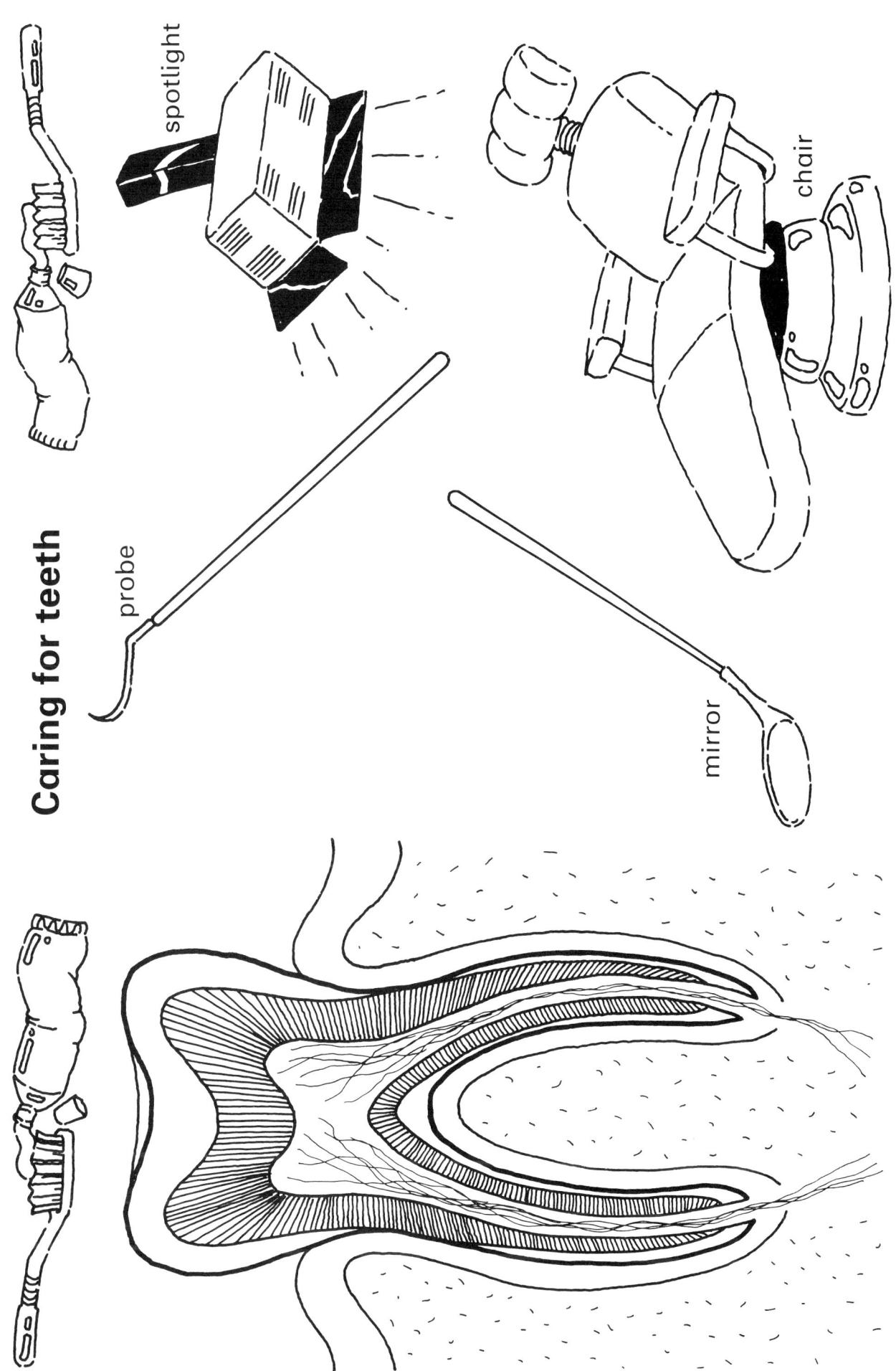

spotlight

probe

mirror

chair

Healing C73

Our healing community

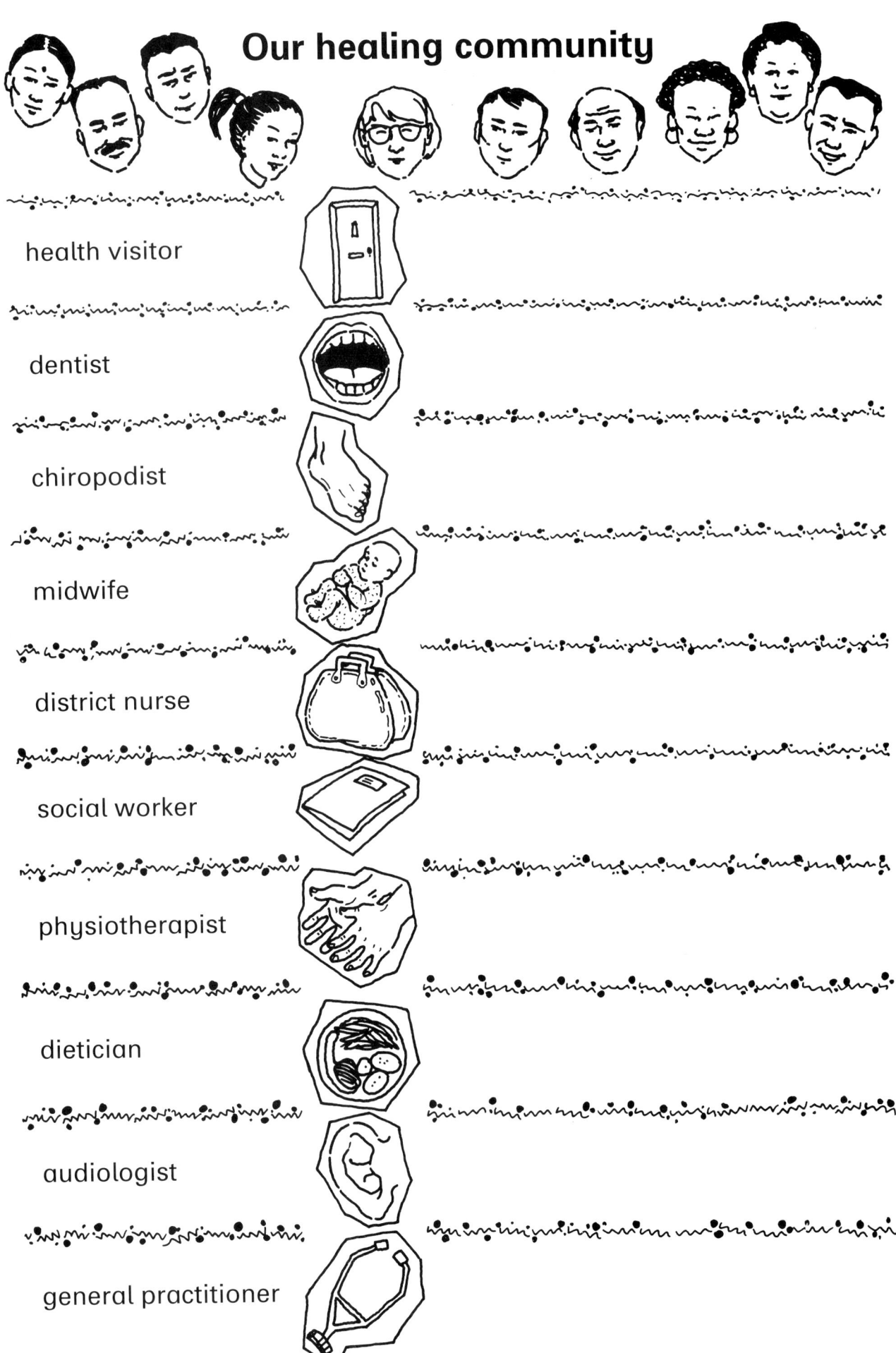

health visitor

dentist

chiropodist

midwife

district nurse

social worker

physiotherapist

dietician

audiologist

general practitioner

106

Healing people jigsaw

smallpox vaccine

Samuel Hahnemann
(1755–1843)

Edward Jenner
(1749–1823)

homeopathic cures

Florence Nightingale
(1820–1910)

X-rays

Louis Pasteur
(1822–95)

rabies vaccine

Wilhelm Konrad Röntgen
(1845–1923)

hospital care

mind investigations

helps the poor
and sick

heart transplants

Sigmund Freud
(1856–1939)

Mother Teresa
(1910–)

Christiaan Barnard
(1922–)

Healing C75

Natural healing card

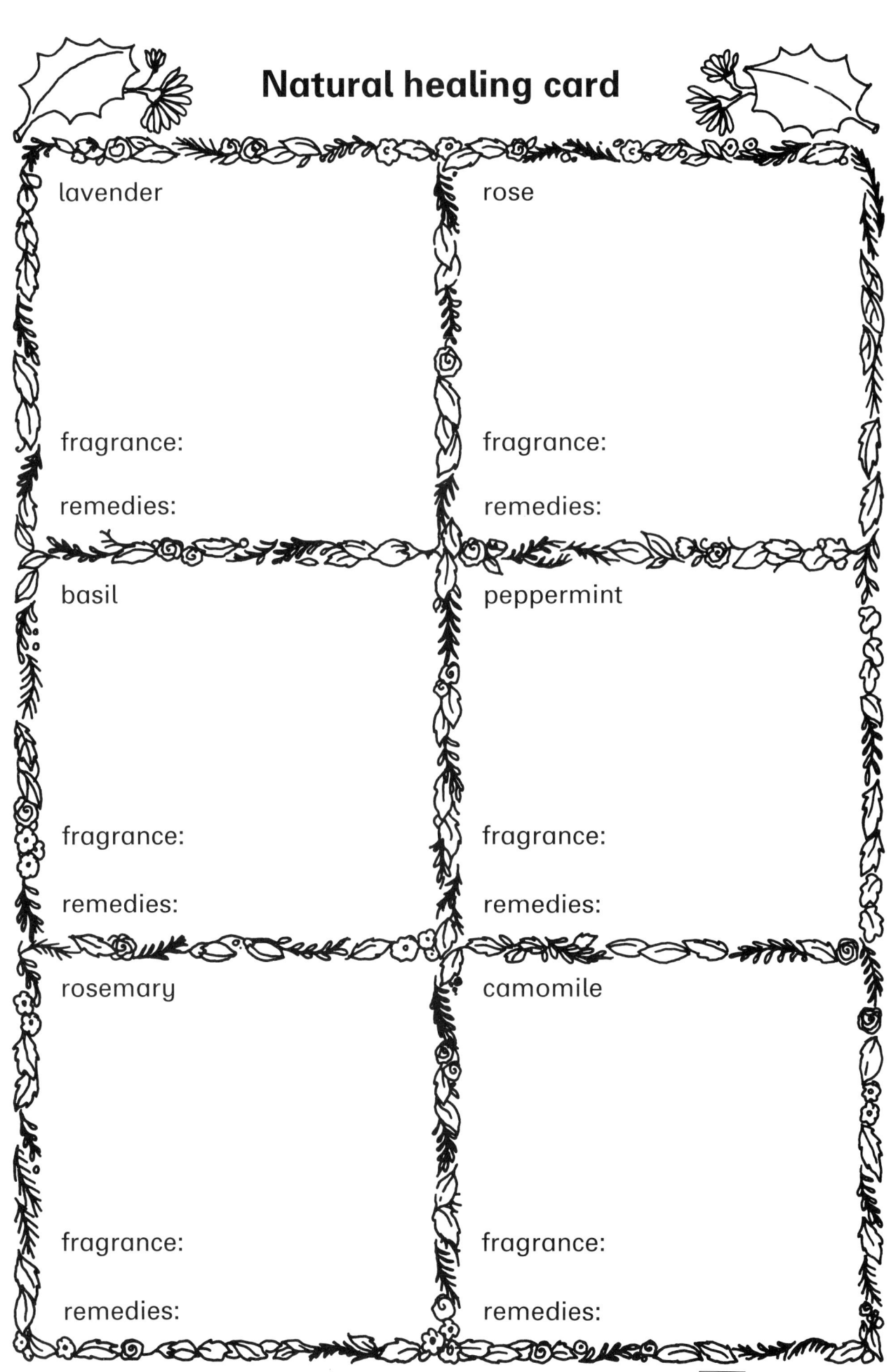

lavender

fragrance:

remedies:

rose

fragrance:

remedies:

basil

fragrance:

remedies:

peppermint

fragrance:

remedies:

rosemary

fragrance:

remedies:

camomile

fragrance:

remedies:

✓ Healing C76

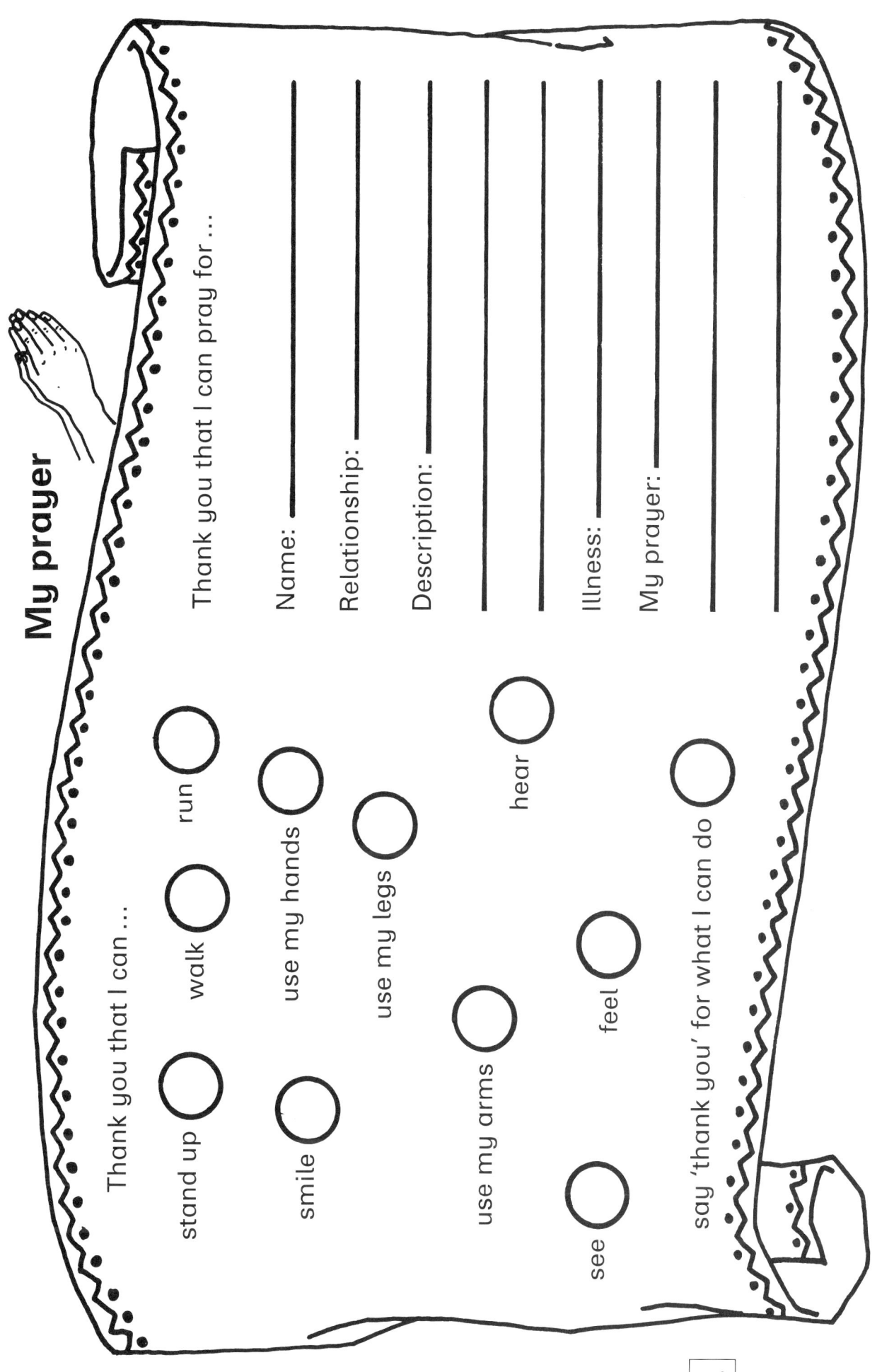

My prayer

Thank you that I can pray for …

Name: _____

Relationship: _____

Description: _____

_____

Illness: _____

My prayer: _____

Thank you that I can …

stand up ◯

run ◯

walk ◯

smile ◯

use my hands ◯

use my legs ◯

use my arms ◯

hear ◯

feel ◯

see ◯

say 'thank you' for what I can do ◯

✓ Healing C77

Jesus the healer

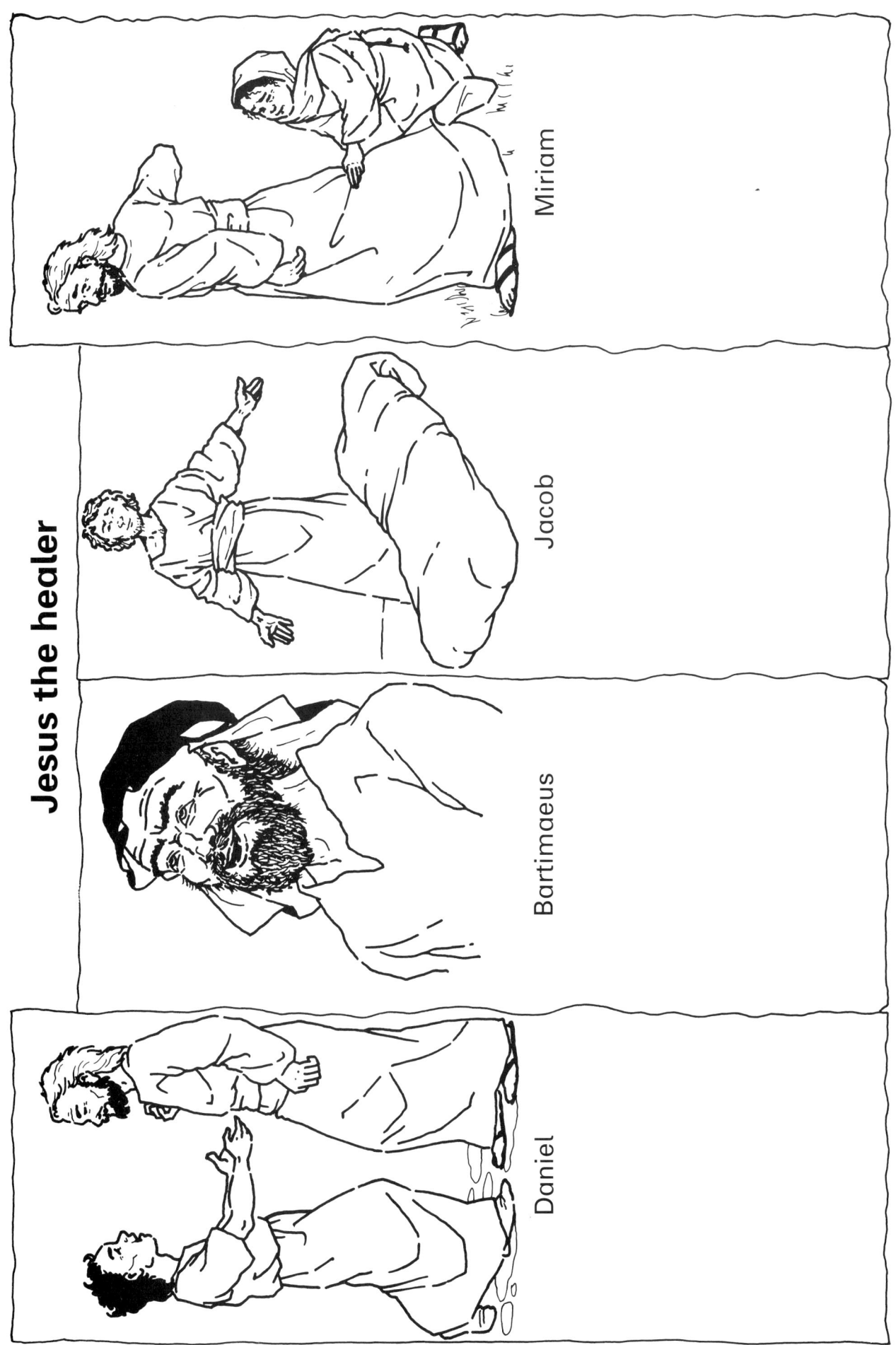

Miriam

Jacob

Bartimaeus

Daniel

Healing C78

Healing miracles

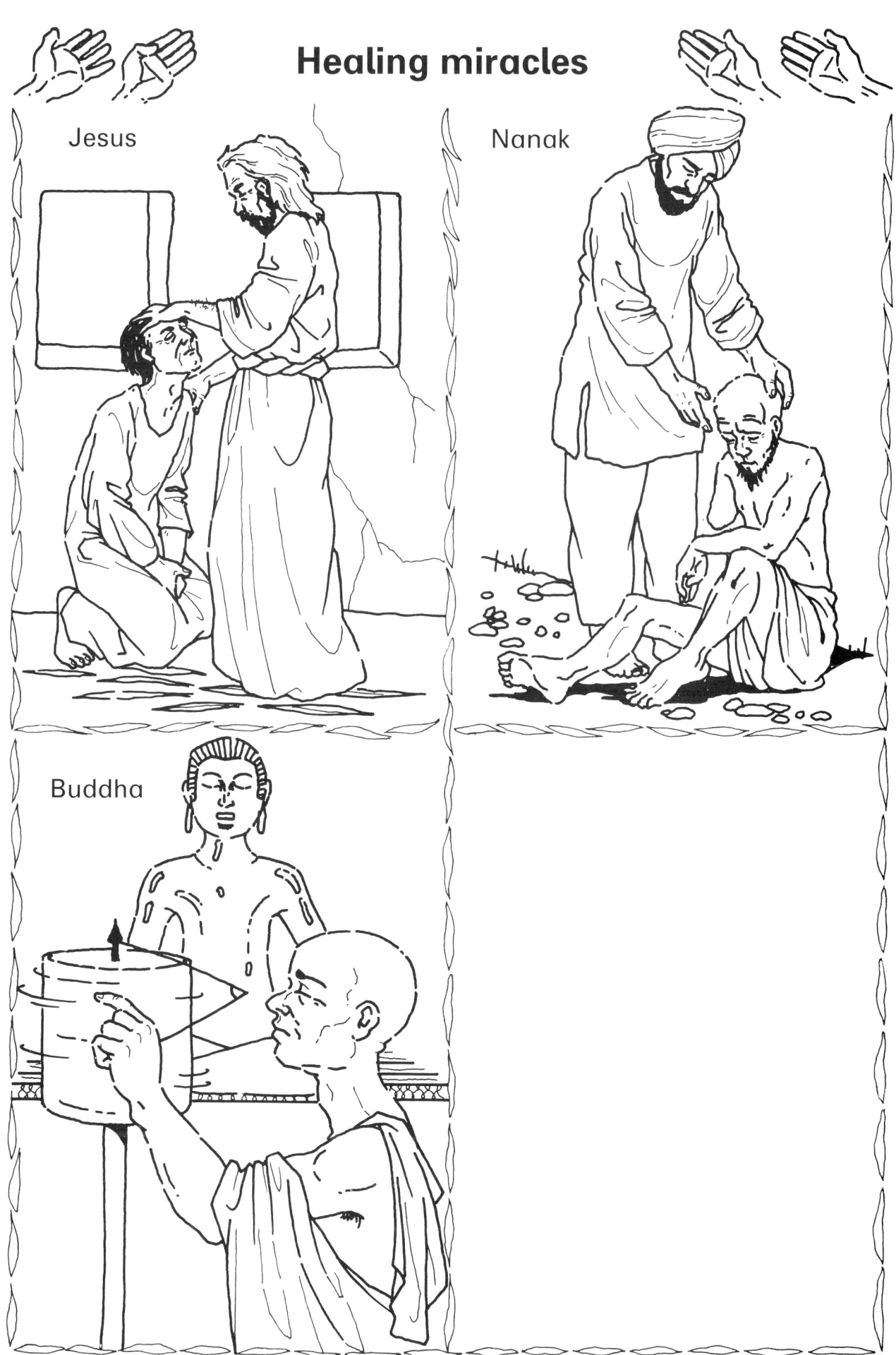

Jesus

Nanak

Buddha

111

a playground fight

a family argument

terrorism

race conflict

My new friend

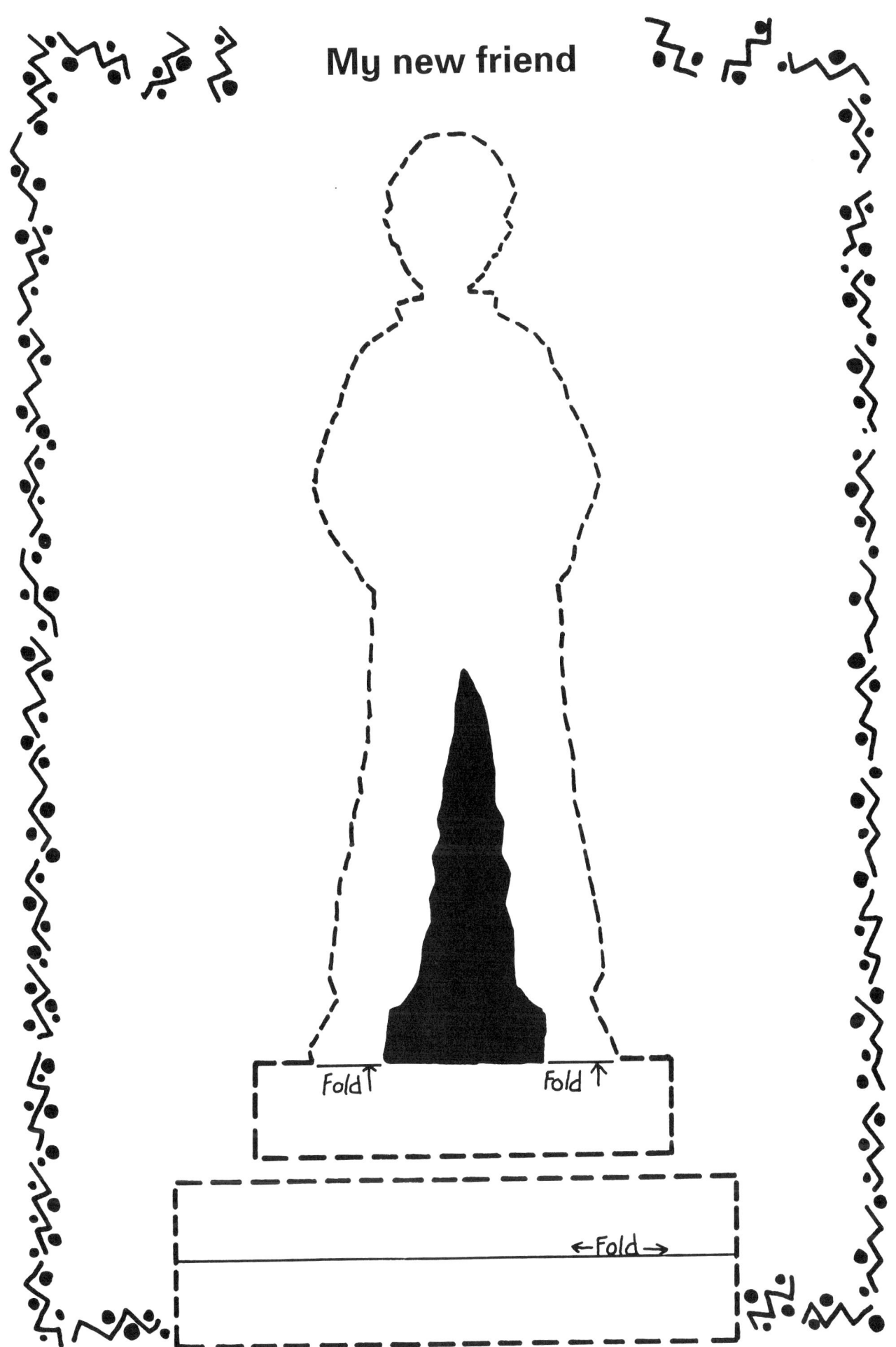

Fold ↑   Fold ↑

← Fold →

Other people count   C81

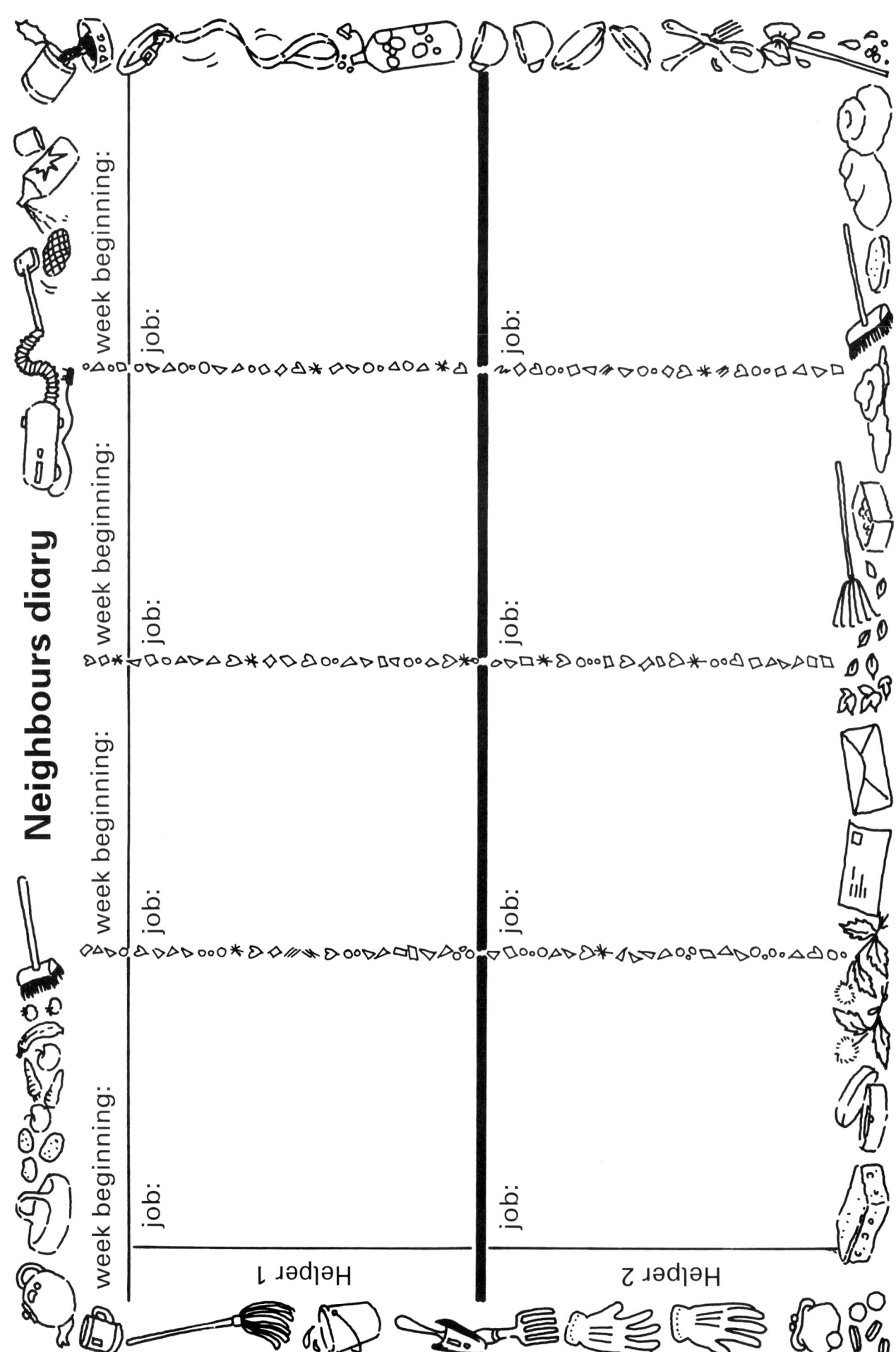

Neighbours diary

	week beginning:	week beginning:	week beginning:
Helper 1	job:	job:	job:
Helper 2	job:	job:	job:

Other people count C82

Global caring

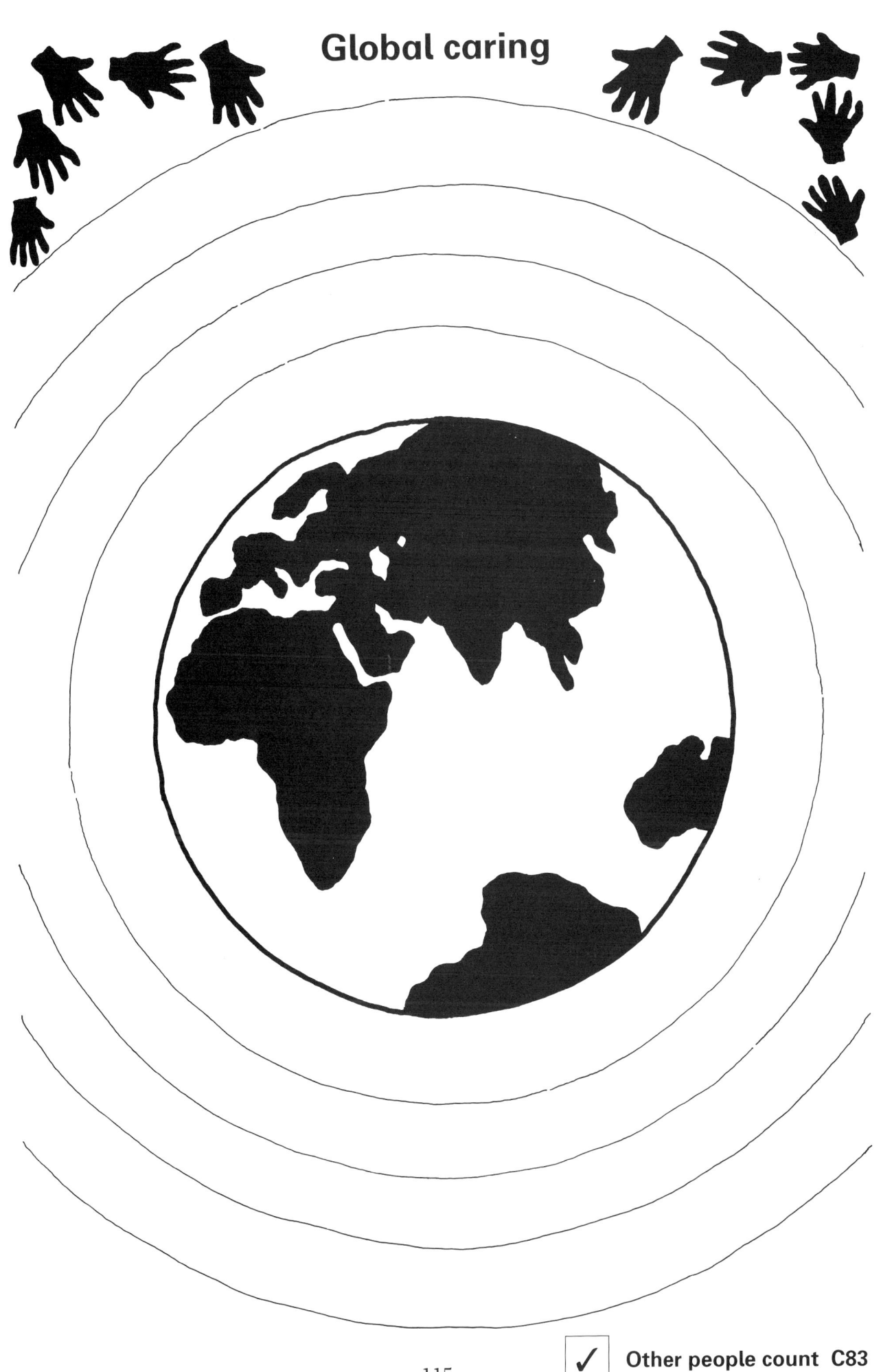

✓ **Other people count C83**

My family cares

name: _____ name: _____

name: _____ name: _____

Things I could do for them:

116

Do I think like this?

often ◯   sometimes ◯   never ◯   often ◯   sometimes ◯   never ◯

often ◯   sometimes ◯   never ◯   often ◯   sometimes ◯   never ◯

often ◯   sometimes ◯   never ◯   often ◯   sometimes ◯   never ◯

✓ Other people count C85

117

Family kindness

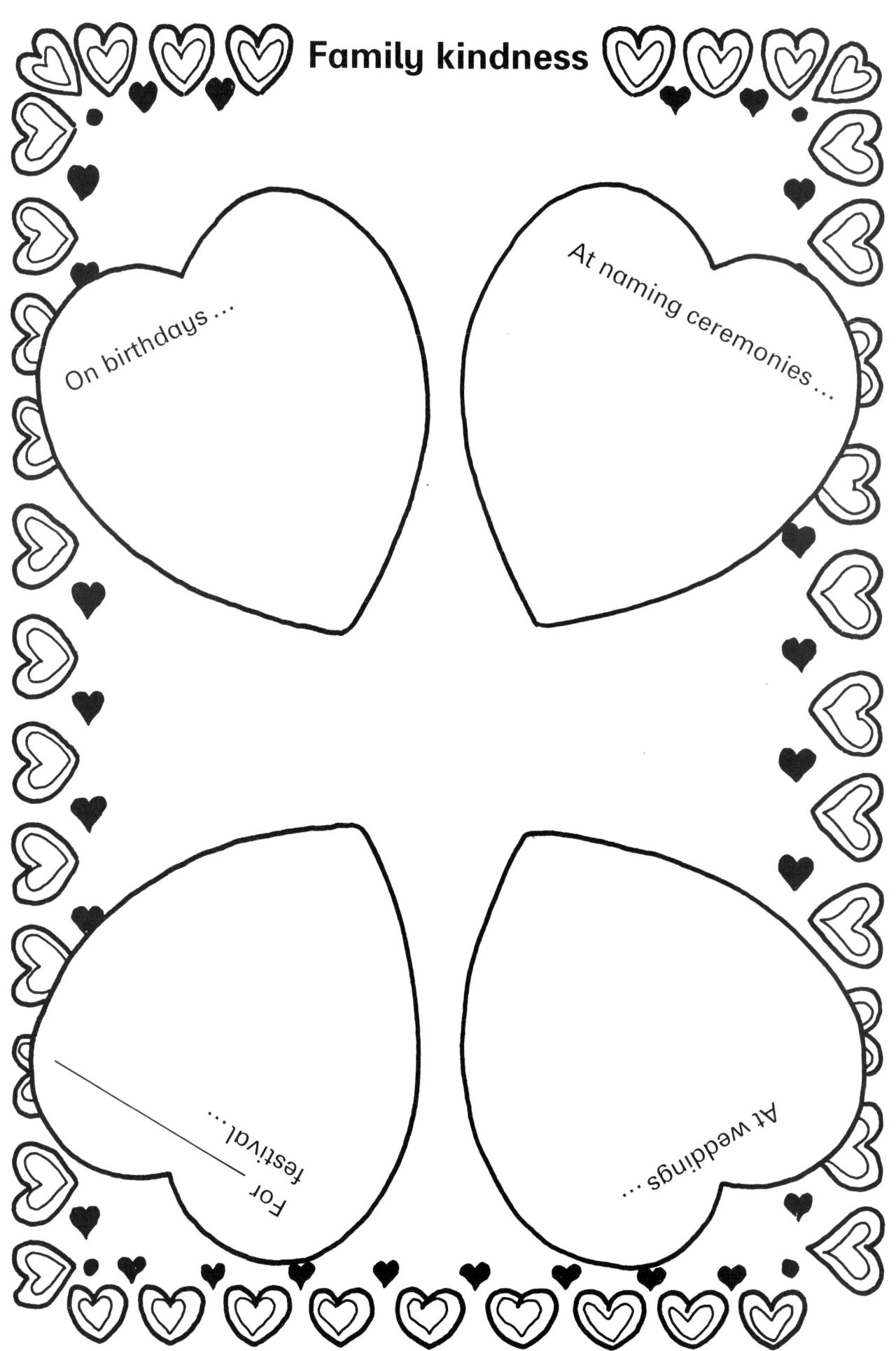

On birthdays ...

At naming ceremonies ...

For festival ...

At weddings ...

Other people count C86

A happy event

Occasion: _____

Date: _____

Time: _____

Place: _____

What I did: _____

_____

_____

Signed: _____

Other people count C87

Zacchaeus counted

fold

fold

fold

120

Other people help

our postman

the police

our lollipop lady

our teacher

my doctor

121

Counting through faith

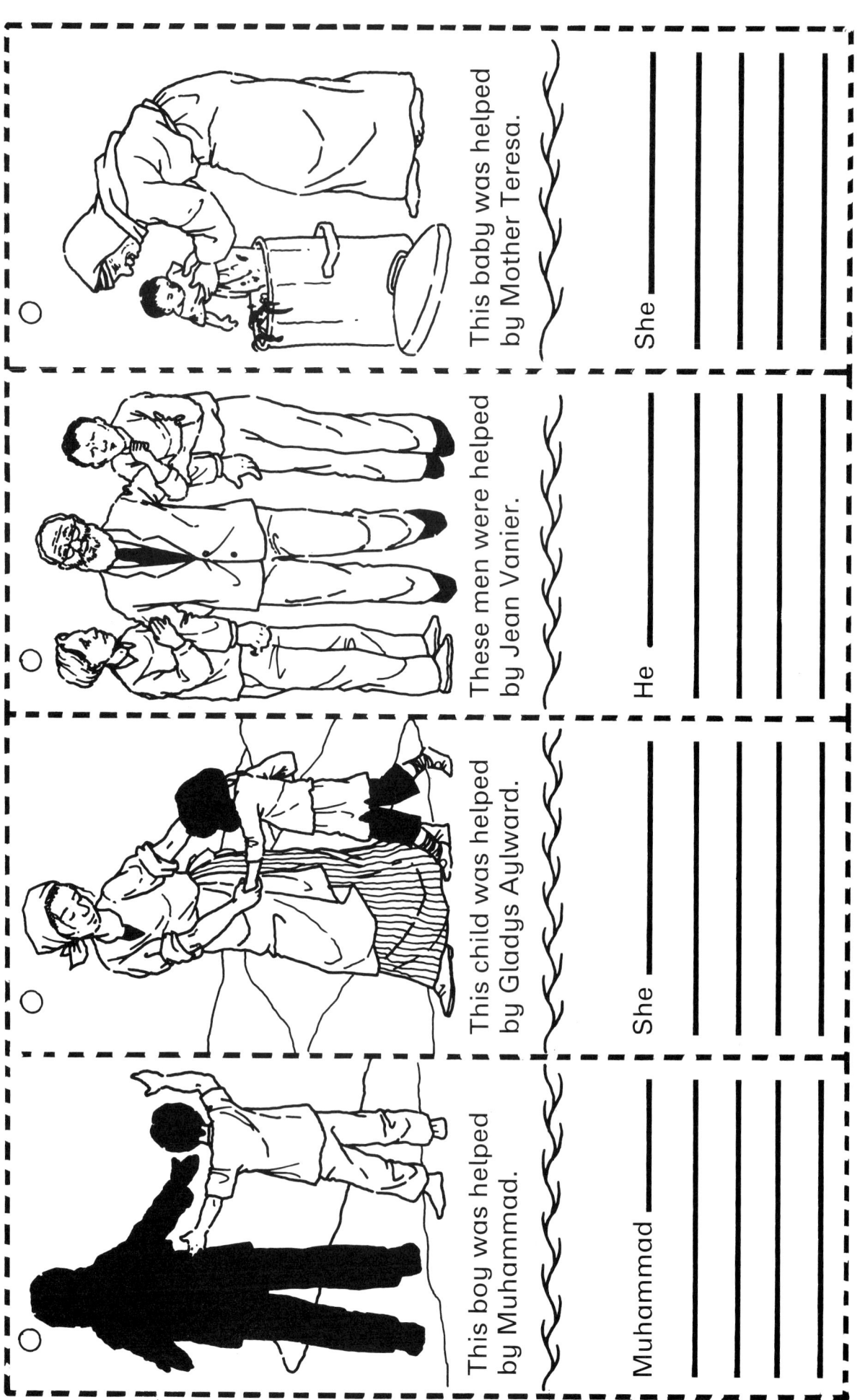

This baby was helped by Mother Teresa.

She _____

These men were helped by Jean Vanier.

He _____

This child was helped by Gladys Aylward.

She _____

This boy was helped by Muhammad.

Muhammad _____

Other people count C90